Charles Vince

Lights and Shadows in the Life of King David

Charles Vince

Lights and Shadows in the Life of King David

ISBN/EAN: 9783337059125

Printed in Europe, USA, Canada, Australia, Japan

Cover: Foto ©Lupo / pixelio.de

More available books at **www.hansebooks.com**

Lights and Shadows

in the life of

King David.

BY

CHARLES VINCE.

LONDON:
ELLIOT STOCK, 62, PATERNOSTER ROW.
1871.

"Men and Brethren, let me freely speak unto you of the Patriarch David."

PREFACE.

THE historical books of the Old Testament are the objects of repeated attacks. One of the best methods of defending them and preserving our belief in them is to use them diligently for practical religious purposes. If our acquaintance with them be very imperfect, and our study of them very infrequent, the spiritual profit we derive must be scanty. The less good we get from them the more difficult it is to maintain a living faith in their Divine authority. On the other hand, the more the histories of Scripture are read, the more it will be seen how true they are to human life and experience; how full they are of revelations of God and man; and how rich they are in lessons of wisdom for all generations. If by using them we find that they are "profitable for doctrine, for reproof, for correction, for instruction in righteousness," it will be no impossible task for us to believe that "they were given by inspiration of God." By their fruits in our own hearts and lives we shall judge them, knowing that men do not gather grapes off thorns, or figs of thistles.

It is with the hope of promoting, in some measure, an increased use of Old Testament histories that the following studies in the life of David are published. Only a few of the incidents of his eventful career have been taken, and these are not more fruitful in instruction than many of those which for lack of space have been left unnoticed. There will be a good recompense for the labour of writing, if what is here written sends its readers to the Bible with the determination to learn afresh all which can be learnt of the man after God's own heart.

The writer is quite aware that in his desire to be always practical, he is sometimes, if not frequently, desultory. Will the readers who blame him for sacrificing the unity of any particular chapter, kindly bear in mind for what purpose the sacrifice was made. The aim throughout has been to show that there is some lesson for to-day in every recorded fact in the life of him who, in such a far-off time, "served his generation by the will of God, fell asleep, and was laid unto his fathers."

CONTENTS.

		PAGE
I.	*THE TWO VICTORIES IN ONE DAY*	1
II.	*DIVINE GOODNESS IN HUMAN FRIENDSHIP*	23
III.	*VENGEANCE LEFT WITH HIM TO WHOM IT BELONGS*	45
IV.	*NABAL THE CHURL*	67
V.	*DIVINE CORRECTION OF A PROPHET'S MISTAKE, AND DIVINE DENIAL OF A KING'S DESIRE*	87
VI.	*GREAT TROUBLES FOLLOWING GREAT TRANSGRESSIONS*	119
VII.	*THE QUICKENING OF DAVID'S CONSCIENCE BY RIZPAH'S EXAMPLE*	141

		PAGE
VIII.	*THE TWO THINGS WHICH DAVID HAD NEVER SEEN*	165
IX.	*THE TWO THINGS WHICH DAVID HAD NEVER SEEN* (*continued*)	187
X.	*THE "LAST WORDS" OF DAVID* . . .	209

I.

THE TWO VICTORIES IN ONE DAY.

1 SAM. xvii. 28, 29; 49, 50.

"And Eliab his eldest brother heard when he spake unto the men: and Eliab's anger was kindled against David, and he said, Why camest thou down hither? and with whom hast thou left those few sheep in the wilderness? I know thy pride, and the naughtiness of thine heart; for thou art come down that thou mightest see the battle. And David said, What have I now done? Is there not a cause?... And David put his hand in his bag, and took thence a stone, and slang it, and smote the Philistine in his forehead, that the stone sunk into his forehead; and he fell upon his face to the earth. So David prevailed over the Philistine with a sling and with a stone, and smote the Philistine, and slew him; but there was no sword in the hand of David."

THE TWO VICTORIES IN ONE DAY.

"THE LORD SEETH NOT AS MAN SEETH." For this fact uncounted multitudes will have reason to rejoice and give thanks for evermore. If the Lord had seen as men saw, David might have been left to spend his long life and to fritter away his great powers in keeping a handful of sheep in the wilderness. When, at the bidding of Samuel, the sons of Jesse were called to the sacrifice, no one thought of sending for David. When the young men were made to pass before the prophet, that he might find amongst them the chosen of the Lord, neither the brothers nor the father of David proposed that he also should be examined. It seems to have been a settled conviction with them all that the youngest of the household could not be the future king of Israel. Not even, when ten of his family had been tried and rejected, did Jesse volunteer the information that he had yet another son. If there had been a conspiracy to frustrate the Divine purpose in relation to David, his relatives could scarcely have kept him out of sight more persistently, or brought him forward more sluggishly and reluctantly. When, a few months later, the wartrumpet sounded throughout the land, and the service of all the brave and strong was needed to resist the invading enemy who had encamped almost beneath the shadows of the mountains that were round about Jerusalem, Jesse sent three of his sons to follow Saul to the battle, but David was not with them. As if no one dreamed of making him a soldier, he was still kept to his obscure labours in the sheep-fold; and the greatest service to which he was called by the voice of man in that season of danger and alarm, was the lowly one of carrying corn and cheeses to his brothers, who were counted able to do something for Israel's deliverance. Men were slow to see the seeds of future greatness and godliness which the Lord beheld, and they looked not for succour in the direction whence He had ordained it to come. Praise belongs to Him for carrying out His own purpose despite the want of discernment and sympathy on the part of His people. If His thoughts had not prevailed over men's thoughts, the Jewish nation would have lost one of its greatest kings, and the Bible one of its most thrilling and instructive histories. The sweet singer of Israel could not have been mute and inglorious; but probably he would have given to mankind little beside quiet pastoral strains, and his Psalms could not have had the wide range and wondrous variety which they owe to his chequered experience, and by which they are so eminently fitted to be the book of praise and prayer for the Church of God in all generations.

The Divine wisdom in the choice of David

was soon proved when the time of trial came, and he had an opportunity of showing the regal spirit the grace of God had given to him. When he entered into the battle-field to begin his soldier-life, he first showed his power in the mastery of himself, and then went on to what was in many respects an inferior triumph—the conquest of Goliath. He bore the revilings of his own brother with meekness, and then, in the same calm and godly mood, he faced the dread foe of his country. It was given to him to achieve two great victories in the same place and on the same day. The second triumph is by far the more famous, but we must not suffer its splendour to hide from us the true glory of the first. The man who kills a giant will always be more talked of than the man who, against the force of strong temptations, controls his own temper; but it is none the less true that—" He that is slow to anger is better than the mighty; and he that ruleth his spirit than he that taketh a city."

I. *David's victory over himself.* He found the

Jewish army headed by a faint-hearted king, and chiefly made up of soldiers who had been suddenly emptied of all courage. Infectious fear had spread through their ranks with greater swiftness and power than a pestilence, and had destroyed both their self-reliance and their faith in God. As soon as the boastful Philistine showed himself in the valley which lay between the two encampments, all the men of Israel fled from him in sore dismay. This was perplexing as well as painful to David, for it did not at all agree with his ideas of godliness or manliness that the hosts of the Lord should turn their backs upon the enemy. He sought to know the matter thoroughly, and was specially anxious to have repeated to him what honours would be given to the man who could roll away the reproach of Israel by the defeat of the bold blasphemer. "And Eliab, his eldest brother, heard when he spake unto the men: and Eliab's anger was kindled against David, and he said, Why camest thou down hither? and with whom hast thou left those few sheep in the wilderness? I know thy pride, and the naughtiness of thine heart; for thou art come down that thou mightest see the battle." It is not difficult to conjecture the cause of Eliab's ill-will and unjust upbraidings. He had not forgiven David for the distinction that God had granted, and the cruel spirit of envy had turned him from a brother into a foe. Was not Eliab rejected and David accepted? and how could the eldest son endure to see the youngest preferred before him? Like Cain, Eliab became implacable, and doubtless hated in his brother the very excellencies for which his God had put such high honour upon him. True, it was Eliab's own brother who was to have the kingdom, but what of that? Nothing would satisfy his envious heart excepting his own possession of the promised greatness. This fiendish passion of envy, so common in human nature, can not only destroy the joy of a brother in a brother's welfare, but would also, if it could get into a mother's heart, be hellish enough to make her miserable at the thought of the prosperity of her own first-born boy. What a foul thing that must be which finds the elements of its own perdition in a sight of the paradise God gives to others, and which would be wretched and wobegone in heaven itself if it met with any one having stronger wings or a higher place than its own!

Eliab might have had fraternal feeling enough to be sorry if any great calamity had befallen David, but his love was not strong enough for the harder task of rejoicing over the bright prospects opened up to his brother by the promises of God. To weep with them that weep requires less true sympathy than to rejoice with them that rejoice. It is often far easier to our fallen natures to be sincerely sorry over the adversity of our neighbours, than to be sincerely and exultingly thankful for the growing greatness of our friends and kinsfolk. Pity for those whom failure has thrust below us can find room in our hearts, when they are too little to contain joy concerning those whom success has lifted above us. We have known Christian men, and ministers too, who, if you were in trouble, would be sure to come with kind words and generous gifts; but, if you were greatly prospered, they would be equally certain to show more or less of a censorious spirit, and find out something to say in disparagement of your prosperity. When Moses lay a helpless babe in the ark of bulrushes, how patiently Miriam waited and watched by the river side! How promptly she did the work assigned to her! and how ingeniously, with the art that conceals art, she suggested that she should be sent to fetch a nurse of the Hebrew women! There was nothing in her manner to awaken suspicion as she ran off to bring back to Pharoah's daughter the babe's own mother! Her sisterly love and anxiety for her imperilled brother made her skilful beyond her years. But when, in after days, God had put great honour upon Moses, and foolish people were jealous of him, Miriam also was carried away and spoke against him, and the Lord smote her with a foul leprosy, a fit symbol of the envy which had broken out upon her soul to defile and disfigure it. When, in the last judgment, Envy is placed at the bar of God, what an indictment will be laid against the Evil Spirit! The insulting anger of Eliab—the cruelty of Joseph's brethren—the murderous wrath of Cain—and the greatest share in the greatest crime in the world, the crucifying of the Lord of glory—will be charged upon him. To cast this demon out of our bosoms before that final condemnation is one purpose of Jesus, and with all our hearts we should pray for His complete and speedy victory.

The taunts and insinuations of Eliab must have cut David to the quick. He had come asking after his brethren's welfare, and making contributions to it, and this was the reward he received for all his kindness. Moved by tender patriotism and piety, he was anxious about the safety of his fatherland and the glory of his God, but his evil-hearted brother put it down to self-conceit and vanity, and denounced, as an instigation of the wicked one, that which David knew to be an inspiration from heaven. If the undeserved rebuke had been administered in private, it would have been hard to bear; but Eliab was base enough to be a public slanderer, and sought, by his foul aspersions, to do irreparable damage to David's reputation amongst those who saw him that day for the first time, and would be too ready to think that there must be good grounds for these charges of pride and arrogance, seeing they were made by the young man's own brother. "Why camest thou down hither?" Eliab asked, with insinuating emphasis, which clearly implied that the avowed purpose of inquiring after and promoting the welfare of his brethren was, on David's part, a mere pretence, and that he was wearing a mask of brotherly kindness in order to hide his own self-seeking and presumption. "With whom hast thou left those few sheep in the wilderness?" was the second evil-suggesting question. "It was not much we cared to confide to you, and even that little you have neglected. I know the pride and the naughtiness of your heart. You may deceive these strangers with your pretended zeal and piety, but you cannot impose upon me." Eliab spoke to David, but, doubtless, it was the listening people he desired to impress with his slanderous talk. He wanted to persuade them that David was utterly unfit for that great work for which he was about to offer himself; and, if the cruel and false words had wrought their intended effect, the people would have certainly refused to commit their cause to the championship of an upstart stripling, against whom even his own brother bore such strong testimony. It would be difficult to imagine a speech which, being of the same length, should breathe more envy and malignity, suggest more falsehood, and be capable of doing more mischief! The temptation must have been strong to answer it with words of burning indignation, and only a man of much meekness and of great self-control could have replied to it as David did. Who likes to be accused of vile motives which he knows have no place in his heart, and to hear his very virtues denounced as being nothing but hideous vices which he tries to conceal by means of pious airs and canting pretensions? And what must it be when the calumny comes from a brother, and the sufferer, pointing to his reputation, pierced with the sharp and poisonous tongue of slander, has to exclaim, with grief too great for tears: "These are the wounds which I have received in the house of my friends." It was a cross of this kind David had to carry, and he bore it as if there had been given to him some prophetic foresight of the perfect example of Him who endured such contradiction of sinners against Himself, and who, when He was reviled, reviled not again.

The restraint which David put upon his temper under this great provocation was the most godly thing he could have done, and therefore it was the wisest and most profitable. Could he have devised a better method of disproving his brother's assertions? If his spirit had flamed forth in angry rejoinder, and if he had publicly branded his brother with the bad names he deserved to bear, the people would probably have found in that so much evidence to sustain Eliab's insinuations. But the gentle spirit and the soft answer turning away wrath must have shown them how much David had been misrepresented. If one be accused of being a great sinner, there is no method of refuting the charge equal to that of manifesting the spirit and maintaining the character of a true saint. "By their fruits ye shall know them. Men do not gather grapes of thorns, or figs of thistles."

Having regard to the great work before him, it was very important that David should keep his temper. Could the second victory have been achieved, if he had failed in the first conflict? His combat with Goliath demanded an undimmed eye, a steady arm, and a calm heart; and, if he had given way to stormy passion for only a brief season, there would have been a lingering feverishness and nervousness utterly unfitting him for the dread struggle on which the fate of two armies and of two nations was depending. His strong faith in God might not have sufficed to give him the necessary quiet and steadiness if he had first suffered fierce anger to disturb his spirit and fill his body with trembling. That which was right amidst the temptations of one hour was the best preparation for the arduous labours of the next hour. All other things being equal, he who is most triumphant over temptation and most faithful to duty to-day, will be the strongest for work and warfare to-morrow. Let God be praised for giving to His servant David the sweet charity which suffereth long and is not easily provoked! Happy they who will not let their souls be easily enkindled by other people's unrighteous anger, but who cultivate a spirit on which insulting words and provoking deeds fall like fire-brands into the quenching sea!

II. *David's victory over Goliath.* History records many instances in which cruelty, and tyranny, and persecution have thoroughly outwitted themselves and frustrated their own purposes. Charity must not rejoice in iniquity, but it may exult in the defeat of iniquity, and especially when iniquity plays the part of a scorpion and stings itself, and when, like Haman, it unwittingly prepares a gallows for its own execution. The defeat of the Philistines in the downfall of their great champion is a most striking illustration of this kind of self-destruction. A few years before the birth of David, the subjugation of Israel by their old enemies was most complete, and the conquerors used their power in such a manner as to make it very unlikely that the crushed people could ever rise again. The whole nation was disarmed, and vigorous measures were used to keep the people from getting any fresh weapons. So abject were the oppressed, and so politic were the oppressors, that every man who followed the occupation of a smith was either put to death or removed to a distance. The roar of the forge, and the ring of the hammer and the anvil, became sounds unknown in Israel; and any Jew who wanted implements for tilling his land or reaping his corn had to go to the Philistines for them. A file was the only tool the

Jew was allowed to have; and when his ploughshare or his axe required more sharpening than the file could give it, he had to take it down to his despotic masters, that with their leave, and by their smiths, it might be made fit for use. This degradation was put upon the Israelites, not only as a sign of their subjection, but also to keep them so destitute of warlike weapons that it would be impossible for them to regain their freedom on the field of battle. "Now there was no smith found throughout all the land of Israel; for the Philistines said, Lest the Hebrews make them swords or spears" (1 Sam. xiii. 19).

This cruel policy was so successful that on one occasion there were only two swords or spears possessed by the entire Jewish army. Saul and Jonathan had them; but all the rest of the people had to use such cumbrous and clumsy weapons as unskilled hands could make without fire or hammer. Necessity has always been the mother of invention, and we may be certain that, when iron weapons were denied to the Hebrews, their skill was largely developed in other directions. The youth of the land could not practise sword-exercise, or learn to poise the spear, and therefore they would be driven to make themselves master. of other methods of defence and assault. Before this period, the Benjamites had become famous for their skill in slinging, for "Among all this people there were seven hundred chosen men left-handed; every one could sling stones at an hair-breadth, and not miss" (Judges xx. 16). When all edged weapons were taken from them, the people would be sure to turn again to those in whose use their fathers had been so renowned, and practice would again make perfect. Slings could be made without forge or anvil, and smooth stones from the brook need not be carried to the Philistine smiths to be sharpened. These facts will satisfactorily account for David's great skill in slinging—a skill which probably he would not have possessed if the Philistines had not driven him to acquire it by denying to him all the more common and convenient implements of war. The closer encounter, which the use of swords would have made necessary, would have put David to a great disadvantage; and it was well for him that he was expert with a weapon which could be used at a distance, so as to prevent Goliath availing himself of his superior stature and strength. Thus the issue proved that the Philistines laid the foundation of their own defeat when they took all swords and spears from the Israelites, and compelled them to try other means of accomplishing their deliverance. The foes of God's people meant it for evil, but God overruled it for good. He brought blessing out of the curse, and made the wrath of man to praise Him. He can make "all things work together for good to them that love Him, to them who are the called according to His purpose."

David's skill with the sling would have failed to gain the victory if it had been divorced from faith in God. It was his trust in the Lord which gave such calmness to his soul, as surely as it was the calmness of his soul which helped to make his arm so steady and his aim so sure. His faith, however, was not a fanatical faith, which violates reason and neglects the most appropriate means. When he refused to wear Saul's armour, he proved his common sense as much as he displayed his confidence in God. His determination to use the sling to which he was accustomed, and not the sword which was strange to him, was the most expedient thing he could do, and, humanly speaking, his only hope of success. A piety like David's will always be careful "to keep the powder dry," as well as "put trust in God." The faith of David was also associated with experience as well as with reason. He remembered past mercies, and thereby encouraged his heart to rest in Him who is ever the same. "The Lord that delivered me out of the paw of the lion, and out of the paw of the bear, He will deliver me out of the hand of this Philistine." His present confidence was the natural fruit of his past gratitude. It is for our good that the Lord bids us be mindful of His mercies, for whoever forgets former deliverances thereby deprives his faith of future nourishment. Those who pass along the road of life, and raise no memorials of Divine goodness, wrong their own souls as certainly as they rob God of His glory. When the greater trials come it is impossible for them to sing that triumphant song of the untroubled spirit—

> "Each sweet Ebenezer I have in review
> Confirms His good pleasure to help me quite through."

Faith always walks with a firmer step when she leans upon the arm of a vigorous and grateful memory. If the terror-stricken soul be tempted to cry out, "Will the Lord cast off for ever? Hath He forgotten to be gracious?" the most effectual way of chasing away despair and regaining confidence is to adopt the Psalmist's resolve—"I WILL REMEMBER THE WORKS OF THE LORD: SURELY I WILL REMEMBER THY WONDERS OF OLD. I WILL MEDITATE ALSO OF ALL THY WORK, AND TALK OF THY DOINGS."

II.

DIVINE GOODNESS IN HUMAN FRIENDSHIP.

PROVERBS xviii. 24.

"There is a friend that sticketh closer than a brother."

DIVINE GOODNESS IN HUMAN FRIENDSHIP.

THE question has often been asked: Whether in these words Solomon was writing history or uttering prophecy? Was he anticipating the goodness and grace of Him who in after-ages should come and display toward men a friendliness more forbearing, patient, unselfish, and enduring than the world had ever heard of before? or was he referring to some man who had already lived and adorned our common nature, and blessed his own circle, with a friendship more generous and constant than the love of a brother's heart? Without denying the prophetic spirit of the proverb, we must contend for its historical character, and for the probability that Solomon was especially referring to his own father's experience. Had he not in mind one or more of those gifted and godly men who at different times were raised up by the Lord to befriend His servant David? The Psalmist received large mercies, and amongst the greatest of Heaven's gifts were the men who helped him in difficulty, defended him in danger, and followed his fortune through all its changing scenes; some of whom stood by him when his own brothers were false to him; and some of whom were loyal and true when his own son played the traitor's part.

In giving these friends God fulfilled His promise, "As thy days so shall thy strength be;" for it was David's good lot to have at different periods of his history friends of different powers and dispositions, and in each period the friend possessed just the opportunities and qualities which made him a gift in season. Jonathan's position, as heir apparent to the throne, his popularity with the people, and his great influence over Saul, combined to make him one of the most valuable friends that David could have had in the days of poverty and persecution and exile. In later years, Nathan's friendship was of just the character that David most required—the friendship of a wise, far-seeing, and inspired man, who could give weighty counsel as to the affairs of the state, and who was too faithful to allow even a king to go unrebuked for his wickedness. Nathan might not have been able to help David much in Saul's court; and it is quite possible that Jonathan would have shrunk from the painful duty of piercing David's strangely callous conscience with the home-thrust, " Thou art the man." How timely was the friendship of the King of Moab, whereby David was able to find shelter for his father and mother in the land of the stranger, when the fact that they were his parents made their own country unsafe for them to dwell in!* By another also what seasonable and suitable friendship was displayed

* 1 Sam. xxii. 3, 4.

in the effort to restrain David from the foolish vengeance and guilty violence on which his heart was set! And in after years, when Jonathan was dead, and Nathan's rebukes were not required, and Absalom's rebellion had put David in danger of starvation, God sent the friends who were most required; for Barzillai, and other men of wealth, came forth to avow their friendship, and to prove it in a manner appropriate to the circumstances of the hour. Thus the Lord was always mindful of His own; and, sending His divine bounties by the hands of human friends, He always made the blessing, and him that brought it, just such as the exigency of His servant demanded—

> "Friends in his mirth, friends in his misery, too;
> Friends given by God in mercy and in love;
> His counsellors, his comforters, and guides;
> His joy in grief, his second bliss in joy."

The highest place of honour amongst David's friends must be given to Jonathan, in whom we have one of the noblest exhibitions of sanctified human nature which the history of the Church records, and by whom there was set an example of friendship which for steadfastness and self-forgetfulness has probably been surpassed only once, and then by Him who in this, as in every other grace and glory of character, is fairer than any of the children of men.

In the account of David's interview with Saul after his great victory, we are told that "it came to pass, when he had made an end of speaking, that the soul of Jonathan was knit with the soul of David, and Jonathan loved him as his own soul." From these words it seems that if Jonathan had seen David before, when he played the harp in Saul's presence, it was only a mere glance, whereby neither the excellencies of one had been discerned, nor the love of the other enkindled. But now Jonathan had witnessed the godly and gallant spirit, the blending of saintly trust and soldierly courage, with which David had gone out to meet Goliath; and he had heard him, as he stood before the king, carrying himself so meekly, and speaking of himself so modestly in the moment of his triumph. As it was faith in God, and not conceit of himself, which had impelled David to enter the lists against the Philistines, so, when that victory was achieved, the uppermost feeling in his heart was not pride of self, but gratitude to God. To cherish thankfulness is a most effective way of destroying vanity, for a man cannot easily flatter himself about that which he knows and feels he owes to the goodness of his God alone. Jonathan recognised in David's spirit and conduct true beauty and nobleness; and therefore, though he was a king's son, and David a poor shepherd-lad, his heart went out to him, glowing with an affection which soon reached the fervour enjoined in the second great commandment, "Thou shalt love thy neighbour as thyself."

In its freedom from all jealousy, Jonathan's conduct was most exemplary. Saul, at first, had some liking for David, and employed him in posts of honour; but the sight of David's growing popularity effectually chilled the heart of the king. As soon as David rose above Saul, and the people gave him first place in their songs, jealousy crept into Saul's spirit, and swiftly changed the shining angel of love into the dark demon of hatred. It was here that the son proved himself to be so much more noble than the father; for Jonathan saw himself surpassed by David, and yet was his faithful friend, and indeed found one reason for his love in that superiority which David had secured. Jonathan was a soldier as well as David, and had won renown on the field before there was any thought of turning the shepherd into a warrior. With only his armour-bearer to accompany him, he had gone amongst the Philistines, and by his cool daring had struck terror into all their hosts, and had achieved a victory which made him the idol of the people—the hero of his generation. How it was that he, who had previously displayed such great courage, did not accept the challenge of Goliath, we cannot tell; but it seems that, for some reason, though he was counted the first man in the army, he was not equal to this new duty. He saw David come forward and do the perilous work; and he knew that he was now no longer the greatest soldier in Israel, but that he must take his place below this shepherd from the wilderness. To his saintly heart this was no insuperable difficulty, for he had greatness and goodness enough to recognise and rejoice in the gifts God had granted to another. As he looked at the victor wearing laurels which he himself ought to have won, he did not say, "David has surpassed me; he has beaten me in my own special path, and I cannot love him:" but he said, "God has been good to this young man, and given him noble qualities, and I will rejoice in his success. I will be grateful for his endowments, and love him because of what the Lord has done for him." We may be sure that Jonathan remembered who had made David to differ, and he would say, "It is the work of infinite wisdom and love, and there is nothing for me but to be glad and to give thanks." This habit of seeing God in everything, what power for good it has! How many virtues it doth nourish, and how many evil things it can restrain! How many bad passions are banished by its influence, like vicious reptiles retreating before the light of day!

The friendship of Jonathan was eminently practical. It did not consist either of fair and flattering words which he uttered, or of a mere luxury of sentiment which he enjoyed. On the very first day of its life it proved its power, by prompting Jonathan to put his royal robes on David's shoulder, to gird his sword on David's thigh, and to place his bow in David's hands; as much as to say, "I will give thee of my best. Thou art more of a king's son than I am. These befit thee more than me." When Saul's envy enkindled hatred, and hatred plotted murder, he whispered his foul purpose to his son and to his servants, and bade them seek for the opportunity of putting David to death. It must have been a sore struggle for Jonathan, filial love restraining him from any undue exposure of his father's wickedness, and faithful friendship impelling him to warn David of his danger. Having put his friend out of harm's way, he went into his father's presence to speak of all the good service David had rendered; and his words were like a shower from heaven falling into the fiery soul of Saul, and, for awhile, subduing the hellish flame which burned so fiercely there, he persuaded his father to take an oath that David should be spared; and, through his intercession, David had his home in the palace once more. In after-days, a like spirit was displayed when a similar danger arose, and, to save his friend, Jonathan braved his father's fury and risked his own life. There are friendships in the world which cost those who cherish them nothing, and like many other cheap things, they are worth just what they cost. The only friendship worth anything in this world is one that can work as well as talk; give as well as weep; cheerfully sustain loss as well as pronounce flattering eulogies. The affection which Jonathan cherished for David proved to be a costly one, but he grudged not the charges.

He acted as if he had anticipated New Testament teaching, or as if some angel from heaven had whispered to his heart the commandment afterwards addressed to the universal Church—"Let us love, not in word, but in deed and truth."

Jonathan's friendship for David was eminently unselfish. It was much that he could do for David; it was but little that David could do for him. Personally, he had no interest in David's continued life and increasing power; but, speaking after the manner of men, his interest lay in the opposite direction. If David were to be king, it would be Jonathan's throne rather than Saul's that he would take. Jonathan was the heir to the kingdom, and all the help he rendered to David was help to the man who would come between him and his inheritance. This was the fact Saul used with such power, and sought to make a firebrand wherewith to set Jonathan's soul all on flame with jealous hatred. "Thou son of the perverse rebellious woman," he exclaimed, "do not I know that thou hast chosen the son of Jesse to thine own confusion? for as long as he liveth upon the ground, thou shalt not be established, nor thy kingdom."* There was force in that appeal which nothing but a strong friendship could have resisted. "What a poor blind fool thou art! Thou art defending the life of thy rival, who will live only to wear the crown that should grace thy head, and to make thee his vassal. Fetch him hither, my son, and let us slay him. It is more for thy sake than mine that I would destroy him; for, if he be spared, thou wilt never be a king like thy father." With how many this reasoning would have prevailed, and this appeal to selfishness have brought out all the worst passions of the heart! The only power it had over Jonathan was to call forth another prayer that David's good deeds might be remembered, and that he might be dealt with according to them. To Saul's selfish heart this nobleness of love and self-forgetfulness seemed nothing but wilful wickedness and sheer madness. How could he comprehend it? As well might a burrowing mole attempt to follow the flight of an eagle, or a croak-

* 1 Sam. xx. 30, 31.

ing reptile sit in judgment upon the skylark's song! Only love can understand love. Hence, "He that loveth not, knoweth not God, for God is love."

Jonathan's friendship had the crowning grace of constancy. It began in the midst of David's newborn popularity, but it lasted through all his reverses. The time came when David was hated at Court, when he was reviled by all who wanted to stand well with the King, and when he was a hunted outlaw at the head of a band of men, many of whom were far from the best in the land. These circumstances must have brought his character under suspicion; and we may be sure that many tongues were set talking against him: but through it all the heart of Jonathan was true as the needle to the pole. The two friends were much separated, and only once for a long season did they enjoy an interview; and then Jonathan spoke with strong confidence and sincere gladness of the certainty of David's exaltation, and dwelt in glowing strains upon the happy future when David should be king, and he be the prime minister. It was evident that

David was losing heart about his own prosperity. Adversity was so lasting, and hope was deferred so long, it is no wonder that his faith became feeble. The constant friend, who before had defended his life, now goes forth to deliver him from despondency, and to bid him rest in the Lord and wait patiently for Him. At the very time that Saul went searching for David to kill him, Jonathan went in quest of him that he might speak words of comfort to him, and keep alive that which was more precious than all besides—his trust in God. "And Jonathan arose, and went to David into the wood, and strengthened his hand in God."* Referring to that visit, "the sweet singer of Israel" might have made this his song :—

> " Much beautiful, and excellent, and fair
> Was seen beneath the sun ; but nought was seen
> More beautiful, or excellent, or fair,
> Than face of faithful friend ; fairest when seen
> In darkest day : and many sounds were sweet,
> Most ravishing, and pleasant to the ear ;
> But sweeter none than voice of faithful friend ;
> Sweet always, sweetest heard in loudest storm."

* 1 Sam. xxiii. 16.

Well might David say, "I am distressed for thee, my brother Jonathan; very pleasant hast thou been unto me; thy love to me was wonderful, passing the love of women!"

There is one fact belonging to this history which has seldom had the attention it deserves. While Jonathan was always faithful to David, he was never false to his father. Some men will cultivate one virtue alone, and make it an Aaron's rod—swallowing up all the other virtues; but this man did not suffer his virtues as a friend to devour his virtues as a son. His position was one of great difficulty, and it was little less than a miracle of grace that he was able to keep the true path, when there was so much to turn him to the right hand or to the left. Here were his father and his friend, and the former counted the latter the greatest foe he had, and fought against him with relentless cruelty! How could Jonathan stand between them both, and be to them what a son and a friend ought to be? But he did it; for he was simple-hearted and pure-minded, and anxious to do right; and to the upright there always ariseth light in the darkness. Amid all the strife and conflict between Saul and David, no one can point to a single incident and say, "*There* Jonathan forgot his friendship for David," or, "*There* he broke the first commandment with promise." He never forsook his father's standard, and he died at last nobly fighting by his father's side. He did not say, "It is the purpose of God to bring David to the throne, and I will go and help him to get it." Nay; for he knew that he was to find his rule of action, not in God's purposes, but in God's precepts, one of which is, "Honour thy father and thy mother, that thy days may be long in the land which the Lord thy God giveth thee." After all, that death on Gilboa was a fitting finish to his career! It was well that he who in life had given the world its greatest example of faithfulness to a friend, should in death show to all sons, down to the end of time, that neither a father's failings, nor even a father's crimes, must be allowed to quench filial affection and fidelity. It was a noble thing in Jonathan, that when sin had come with its desolating hand and destroyed all the beauty and glory in his father's character, he carried himself as one who would say, "He is my father still; I will live for him; and, if need be, I will die for him."

It needs no word to prove that the friendship we have been studying must have been a great help and blessing to David. How great, is known only to Him by whom the boon was bestowed. We are told that at the foot of the Hill of Difficulty, a fountain is placed by the Lord of the Pilgrims, so that they may drink and be refreshed before they begin to climb. That is Bunyan's way of putting the fact, that for special circumstances special grace is given; and such a fountain at the foot of David's hill of difficulty was the friendship of Jonathan. Great trials were before him, and God, who foresaw them all, granted him this provision against them. When his character was traduced, how it would solace him to remember that the second man in the land in point of worldly position, and the first man in the land in point of spiritual life, still believed in him and counted him worthy of all love!

When his own heart sunk with fear, there would be reviving power in the thought that such a godly man as Jonathan had the utmost confidence that he would be raised to the throne. We are strangely constituted, and sometimes other people's faith in our future welfare serves us to lean upon when we have none of our own to sustain us. The promises of God concerning us seem sweeter and purer, when, instead of being left to whisper them ourselves to our troubled spirits, we have some believing friend to come and quote them to us.

As we contemplate the character of Jonathan, we are made increasingly thankful that the immortality of the good is revealed in God's Word beyond the possibility of doubt or question. Who would like to believe that when the body of Jonathan fell in the field by the sword of the Philistines, there was an end to all his virtues? Who could believe that the great and glorious saintliness which Divine grace had built up did then and there utterly perish? Surely, God our Saviour did not create such beauty of holiness only that it might be speedily annihilated! Did He not call it into being with the purpose of maintaining it in perpetual vigour, and investing it with power of unlimited progress? Did He not remove it from these lower scenes that He might touch it into a diviner perfection, and have it near Himself for joy and glory evermore?

> "And, doubtless, unto thee is given
> A life that bears immortal fruit,
> In such great offices as suit
> The full-grown energies of heaven."

Yes! we are forbidden to think that the love of Jonathan's heart, which wrought so beneficently on earth, labours no longer for the welfare of others. Can it be possible that the God who created it in His own image doomed it to indolence? Would not that be to doom the possessor of it to misery? How can those who are gifted with a divinely generous nature be happy, if no service of benevolence be assigned to them? As none can imagine to what colossal stature the love of Jonathan has grown in the congenial atmosphere of heaven, so none can imagine in what gladdening and glorious ministries it has been employed. It is as true of the *work* of eternity as it is of its *rest*, "Eye hath not seen, nor ear heard, neither have entered into the heart of man, the things which God hath prepared for them that love Him." But this we know, that He who gives His children the desire to do good to others, can open before them an infinite variety of ways wherein their desire may be gratified.

> " Nor blame I death, because He bare
> The use of virtue out of earth ;
> I know transplanted human worth,
> Will bloom to profit otherwhere."

III.

VENGEANCE LEFT WITH HIM TO WHOM IT BELONGS.

---

1 Samuel xxiv., xxvi.

VENGEANCE LEFT WITH HIM TO WHOM IT BELONGS.

OUR attention has been called to the fact that the first great victory achieved by David was over his own spirit. He kept himself meek and gentle when the shamefully unjust insinuations and charges of his brother presented a strong temptation to be hot in temper and hasty in speech. . As we pursue his history, we are glad to find that his first triumph of this noblest kind was not his last. The grace whereby he achieved the first abode with him still, and enabled him to win a yet more glorious victory. In the scenes brought before us by the two chapters indicated on p. 45, we see him restraining wrath, and exercising mercy, at a time when the inducements to taste "the sweetness of revenge" were many and powerful. His cruel and implacable foe, who had come out with three thousand armed men determined either to take him prisoner or to hunt him to death, was now entirely in his hands. It was a golden opportunity, and David made a golden use of it, for he refused to avenge himself, and suffered his deadly enemy to depart in peace. Behold the man after God's own heart! Let us draw near and look more closely into this deed of saintly magnanimity, and listen to the benediction which the voice of God pronounces upon it: "Blessed are the merciful, for they shall obtain mercy."

If we would fully appreciate the nobleness of David's conduct, we must glance at the circumstances in which he was placed, and the experiences through which he had recently passed. For three years he had lived the life of a fugitive, and in many ways and places had sought to shelter himself against the unrighteous and pitiless wrath of Saul. Once he flew to Ramah, where Samuel lived, and there, telling the tale of his troubles, he received from the aged prophet all the counsel and sympathy and consolation which his circumstances demanded, and for which his heart yearned. In the home and under the protection of Samuel, he found for a brief season a peaceful resting-place, but it was not long before the sleepless hostility of Saul drove him out of that sanctuary. Like the mariners, who exclaim, "It is better to put into any port than be destroyed by the storm," David next betook himself to a strange hiding-place. He went out of his own country, amongst the idolatrous Philistines, whose champion he had slain, whose pride he had humbled, and whose power he had broken. The persecutions of Saul had brought him into such a plight, that he was safer amongst his "natural enemies" than amongst his own people; and it was better for him to cast himself on the generosity of those who had many reasons for being hostile to him, than to brave the anger of the King whom he had faithfully served, and by whom he was hated without a cause. The security David enjoyed amongst the Philistines was short-lived, and he soon had to seek shelter elsewhere. Returning homewards, the weary wanderer took refuge in the cave of Adullam, where he was joined by a number of men, some of whom were of little credit to him, and the government of whom must often have been a great trouble to him. The power which was brought him by the accession of these men, he speedily used in a most praiseworthy manner. It appears that the persecutions of Saul were extended from David to his father and mother, and hence Judæa was no longer a safe land for Jesse and his household to dwell in; and one of the first purposes to which David put his newly acquired strength was that of carrying them beyond the reach of danger. Guarding them with the shields and swords of his fugitive warriors, he took them over the mountains to Mizpeh of Moab, and said to the King of Moab, "Let my father and my mother, I pray thee, come forth, and be with you till I know what God will do for me." If one were disposed to paint a series of pictures illustrative of the fact that David was a man after God's own heart, he might wisely take this scene as one of the subjects of his illustrations. Was David ever more truly and more fully the man after God's own heart, than when he came out of his stronghold, and risked his own life and liberty, in order to secure the peace and comfort of his imperilled parents? That surely was a deed of filial reverence and love which went up for a memorial before Him who made this the first commandment with promise, "Honour thy father and thy mother: that thy days may be long in the land which the Lord thy God giveth thee."

The anger of Saul still burned against David as fiercely as ever, and proved its relentless cruelty by consuming an entire city of consecrated men, because one of their number had given bread to David and his followers, when he supposed them to be still in the King's service. The only respite David enjoyed was, when the invasion of the country by a foreign foe, or some other great exigency, made it impossible for Saul to employ his time and his forces in hunting down a solitary adversary. Once and again, Saul was called from his pursuit of David by some state emergency; but as soon as the Imperial trouble had passed away, he returned with the fury of a monomaniac to his wonted work of worrying the son of Jesse into the grave. At last he went forth with three thousand picked men, and it must have seemed impossible for any earthly power to come for a long season between him and the gratification of his malice. David and his band went for safety into a great cavern which stretched so far into the sides of the mountain that its innermost recesses were dark as midnight, and vast enough to hide a thousand warriors in their gloom.* In

* "The wilderness of Engedi is everywhere of limestone formation, and has its surface broken into conical hills and ridges, from two hundred to four hundred feet in height. On all sides the country is full of caverns, which serve as lurking

this darkness David and his followers concealed themselves; and doubtless they did not venture to break the silence by a single word, and were almost afraid to breathe, lest the slightest noise should betray them; for if they had been discovered, their position would have been one of utter helplessness, as with his superior forces Saul could have turned their hiding-place into a prison, and easily starved them to death, or forced them to surrender. Presently the sultry hour of noontide came, and the King sought a shelter from the burning sky, and a place of quiet for that midday repose which the exhausting heat of Eastern lands makes so necessary. Not "as chance would have it," but as the providence of God ordained it, he went to enjoy his *siesta* in the mouth of the very cavern wherein David and his men were hidden. We can scarcely conceive, much less describe, the breathless interest, the agony of earnestness, with which

places for outlaws at the present day. Some of these can easily give shelter to 1,500 men."—*Kitto.*

they watched and witnessed all that was taking place. Looking from the darkness that made them invisible toward the daylight, they could see the King wrap himself in his robes, and compose himself to sleep, unconscious of the dread danger that was so close to him. David's men deemed this to be the favourable opportunity for him to free himself from all trouble by a single thrust of his sword, and they vehemently urged him to avail himself of it. But the Lord was with him, and filled his heart with mercy instead of revenge, and held him back from the violence to which so many things impelled him. He heard and heeded the voice Divine, "Vengeance is mine, I will repay, saith the Lord. If thine enemy hunger, feed him; if he thirst, give him drink. Be not overcome of evil, but overcome evil with good."

This brief review of David's circumstances will suffice to show that there were many things to enkindle his resentment and make forbearance towards Saul a most difficult virtue. Think of what he had lost, and what he had suffered! He was young and brave and richly gifted, and eminently fitted for the highest duties and purest joys of social life; but for three years he had been hunted like a wild beast, as if he were a curse to the earth, utterly unfit for the haunts of men, and worthy only of being a target for Saul's archers to shoot at. Sometimes he had been doomed to dreary solitude, and at other times he who would have graced the highest and holiest circles in the land had been obliged to make himself the bosom-companion of demoralised debtors and discontented outlaws, many of whom mistook the proper object of their indignation, and were angry with society instead of condemning themselves. He was endowed by nature, and set apart by Providence, for great service to the state, and, after a season of useful disciplinary obscurity and lowly labour, he came forth to publicity and fame. Life opened out gloriously before him, and he had the fairest prospect of attaining to true greatness by serving his generation according to the will of

God. Suddenly his sky was completely overcast, and the cup of sweet hope was dashed from his lips; and he who possessed unsurpassed powers for helping his country was forced to hide himself among its enemies, or make himself the leader of its outcasts. What had brought all this to pass? No court of justice had passed sentence upon him. No council of the nation had consigned him to banishment. The people had not cast him off. The Lord God had not forsaken him. All this loss and sorrow and evil had come upon him through the unprovoked anger of one man's heart, and now that man lay helpless at his feet. Verily the devil stood on high vantage ground that day, when he tempted David not to forgive his enemy, but to slay him in his sleep!

It was not only what Saul's death would deliver David from, but also what it would introduce him to, that had to be considered. The consecrating oil had been poured upon his head, and one of the greatest of God's prophets had hailed him as future King of Israel; and if Saul were out of the way, the chief if not the last barrier between him and the throne would be gone. It would be no light thing to exchange the caves of the mountains for the palaces of Jewry, and the life of a hunted outlaw for the life of a king revered and obeyed, and surrounded with all that power could procure or wealth could purchase. According to man's code of morals, it would have been neither murder nor manslaughter, nor any other crime, to put Saul to death, for he had declared war against David, and had come out against him with vastly superior forces. If David had slain him, and thus have cleared his own way to the kingdom, how many would have praised the deed! The voices that persuaded him to do it were many and mighty, some of them must have sounded like angel-voices, and it was almost a miracle of grace that the one voice of conscience was strong enough to outcry them all.

The tempter is never so likely to succeed, as when he transforms himself into an angel of light, and makes the real sin look so much like a virtue that it is difficult to discern the deception. This he did in David's case, speaking through David's men, and trying to convince him that the opportunity to avenge himself was a boon which heaven had sent him in fulfilment of a promise the Lord had made to him. "*And the men of David said to him, Behold the day of which the Lord said unto thee, Behold I will deliver thine enemy into thine hand, that thou mayest do to him as it shall seem good to thee.*" How strangely things combined together to make the worse appear the better course! The promise and the providence of God both seemed on the side of instant and complete vengeance! But David was versed in the Law of God; and in one of the earlier books of his incomplete, but precious, priceless Bible, he had read these commandments: "*Thou shalt not avenge nor bear any grudge against the children of thy people, but thou shalt love thy neighbour as thyself:* I AM THE LORD."* He knew that man must shape his course by the precepts of God, and must never violate any Divine law

---

* Lev. xix. 18.

with the notion that thereby he can bring about the fulfilment of Divine promises and purposes. Man's duty ever is, to believe the promises, to obey the commandments, and to leave the fulfilment of the promises to Him who has made them, and who is always strong enough to keep them, and too faithful to forget them.

David's generous forbearance touched the heart of Saul, disarmed him of his rage, melted him into tears, and constrained him to become a suppliant at the feet of the man for whose blood he had been thirsting. In Saul's profuse professions of good-will, David placed as much confidence as they deserved—none at all. David would be merciful, but that was no reason why he should be foolish, and forego all prudence; so, when Saul went away to his palace, he betook himself to his stronghold again. The generous mood of the King was as brief as the sunshine of a wintry afternoon, and he soon suffered his wrath to drive him into renewed hostilities. A second time he fell into David's hands, and was allowed to escape unhurt. This second display of magnanimity on David's part was a greater triumph of saintly principle than the first. All the former reasons in favour of avenging himself still existed, and in greater force, because of the additional sufferings he had endured; and now there was to be added another reason of almost irresistible power. He had cast his pearl before swine which had turned again to rend him. His kindness had been shamefully abused, and evil had been returned for his good. The King's life, which he had nobly spared, was consecrated afresh to the work of securing his destruction. To spare it a second time was for David to sharpen the sword by which he himself would be slain; and that surely would be charity degenerating into fanaticism. More than ever the tempter that spoke in favour of revenge looked and spoke like an angel of light; but the God whom David desired to obey gave his servant strength equal to his day, and once more, though the forces in favour of evil were a great host, the victory was on the side of godlike forbearance and forgiveness. This lesson the history teaches most plainly and powerfully, that when the saint is watchful and prayerful, and enjoys the Divine succour which watchfulness and prayer cannot fail to secure, there is no temptation too strong for him to resist, and there is no difficulty in the practice of holiness too great for him to surmount. He can do all things through the Lord who strengtheneth him.

It is evident that David's faith in God was one of the great roots out of which all these fruits of forbearance and patience and compassion grew. He was confident that God would in His own way and in His own time fulfil the promises which had been made; and, therefore, instead of taking the matter into his own hands, he could rest in the Lord and wait patiently for Him. What a contrast between his conduct and that of Rebecca! She knew that the promise of God was in favour of her younger son inheriting the place and privileges of the elder, but she could not wait with the patience of faith for God to bring it about in the right way. She pressed falsehood into her service, and taught her child to deceive his own father; and so mother and son conspired together, and tried to carry out the purpose of God by the use of arts learnt from the devil. They did not truly believe, and therefore they made haste. They broke God's laws in order to help on the fulfilment of God's promises, and thereby they mingled for themselves a great and bitter cup of remorse and anguish, the drinking of which extended over many years. David, on the contrary, was determined to do right and leave results with God, and thereby he gained the happy experience which enabled him to say, "In keeping Thy commandments there is great reward." In due season the promise was fulfilled, and he had no memories of unbelieving hastiness and sinful revengefulness on his part to mar the sweetness of the overflowing joy-cup which the goodness of the Lord put into his hands. "*It is good that a man should both hope and quietly wait for the salvation of the Lord.*"

They say that "Revenge is sweet." There can be no doubt of the truth of this, for perverted natures have perverted tastes, and loathe what they ought to love, and banquet with delight on what they ought to abhor. David had feelings in his heart which would have been intensely gratified if he had taken vengeance on his enemy; but would not his revenge have been like the book the seer did eat in the Apocalypse, sweet in the mouth, but bitterness in the belly? If we thought only of present gratification, we might eschew all forbearance and mercifulness, and feast our corrupt tastes with all possible anger and violence against our adversaries; but if we will think of the future, and lay up pleasant memories to be enjoyed in the long hereafter, the less we partake of "the sweetness of revenge," the better. Patience and meekness and forgiveness are often very hard to exercise, but when they become matters of memory, are they not things of beauty, and a joy for ever? The poet tells of one who sat by the grave of the friend from whom he had parted in anger, and wept at the remembrance of his former harshness:—

> "Cruel, cruel the words I said!
> Cruelly come they back to-day."

Probably there are men now sleeping in the dust who in their lifetime wronged and injured you. If you forgave them, and prayed for them, and sought to bless them, does the memory of that Christlikeness on your part ever give you a moment's sorrow? The earthly crown that David gained was torn from his brow long ages ago; but what of his triumph over malice and wrath and uncharitableness? Is not the remembrance of that a part of the feast of bliss of which he partakes in paradise? Does not gratitude to God for that enter into the song he is now singing in heaven? Yes, revenge may be sweet, but like all the pleasures of sin, it is but for a season. Mercy is God's delight. He who receives it through Jesus, secures his passport to the skies. He who learns to imitate it, lays up treasure for himself in heaven. Happy he who by the grace of God so carries himself toward them that curse him and despitefully use him, that he does not invoke his own condemnation, when, in his daily prayer, he cries, "Forgive us our trespasses as we forgive them that trespass against us."

IV.

NABAL THE CHURL.

1 Samuel xxv.

NABAL THE CHURL.

DAVID never made a wiser choice, and he never said a truer thing, than when he exclaimed, "Let us fall now into the hand of the Lord, (for His mercies are great,) and let me not fall into the hand of man." The wisdom and the truth of this were confirmed by more than one incident in David's life, and sometimes the proof was found in his own conduct. As the deeds of others often made him feel, so his purposes and actions must have occasionally made others feel, how much better it was to be cast upon the mercies of God, than to be left to the generosity and forbearance of men. The history of David's collision with Nabal furnishes us with a twofold confirmation of the truth of David's assertion and the wisdom of his decision. David, in a season of feebleness, sought to rest himself upon Nabal's gratitude, and he found that he was trusting in the staff of a broken reed which pierced him. In his necessity he made an appeal to Nabal's generosity, and he found it was as vain as trying to quench his thirst with the waters of Marah. On the other hand, Nabal's ingratitude and unkindness met with no charity at first on the part of David. While Nabal was utterly destitute of brotherly kindness, David failed for a time in the love which is not easily provoked. Because Nabal was insolent as well as thankless, David was carried away by a revengeful spirit, and gathered up all his strength to punish the insult and the wrong with instant death. As David saw his men returning from Nabal empty-handed, and bearing on their lips the cruel answer of the churl,—and as Nabal saw David coming with armed men bent on taking vengeance,—might not each of them appropriately cry out, "Let me not fall into the hand of man?" As we mark the selfish spirit of the wealthy man, and the unforgiving spirit of the wronged man, are we not constrained to exclaim with fresh fervour, "Whether it be for the relief of our necessities, or for the pardon of our transgressions, let us fall now into the hand of the Lord, for His mercies are great"?

The brief account which is given of Nabal's ancestry, and prosperity, and domestic circumstances, prepares us for a description of his character very different from that which the truthful historian supplies. Everything around him was calculated to make him a happy, thankful, sweet-tempered, and kind-hearted man. He had good blood in his veins; and by the memories of his noble and godly ancestor he ought to have been restrained from all that was mean and graceless. He was a descendant of Caleb, the man who stood firm in his faith and obedience at a time when, with one other exception, all the people fell away from their confidence in God and their consecration to His service. He inherited the fruit of the industry and piety of those who had gone before him, and he was unquestionably richer in worldly goods, because he succeeded to devout and diligent men whom the Lord God of Israel had blessed in their labours. The inspired writer alludes to his ancestry as if that increased the guilt of his conduct. "He was of the house of Caleb;" but he was a bad branch growing out of a good stock, for "he was churlish and evil in his doings." Alas! he was neither the first nor the last of those who have come into possession of many of the temporal results of their fathers' piety, but have shamefully repudiated the godliness which brought the golden harvest. They have stood on high vantage ground because they were the sons of "parents passed into the skies," and yet they have scorned and spurned the very religion to which alone their social elevation was owing. Men are often heard to speak of the "good family" to which they belong, as if that justified pride and exclusiveness. The Bible puts it in a different way, and makes the nobleness of a man's ancestry one more reason why he should serve the Lord and cleave to Him with full purpose of heart. The prophet Jeremiah went with words of sharp rebuke and heavy condemnation to one who was proving himself a degenerate son of a godly sire, "Did not thy father eat and drink, and do judgment and justice, and then it was well with him? He judged the cause of the poor and needy; then it was well with him: was not this to know me? saith the Lord. But thine eyes and thine heart are not but for thy covetousness, and for oppression, and for violence, to do it."

Nabal had what many would deem a far more substantial reason for personal goodness than the fact that he belonged to the house of Caleb. The wealth which had come down to him had evidently been increased by the Divine blessing on his own endeavours, and he stood forth conspicuous above all his neighbours for the splendour and luxury with which he could surround himself. "The man was very great," but his prosperity hardened his heart and filled his spirit with haughtiness. It seemed as if the more he got, the more he would spend upon himself, and the less he would be moved with generous sympathy toward those who were in woe or want. Apart from experience, we should deem it impossible that with expanding resources men could become more contracted in liberality; and yet how many have associated a diminished benevolence with doubled or trebled incomes; yea, have given less cheerfully when their power to give was fourfold greater than it had been aforetime. The widow who had less than a pauper's purse, and more than a princely generosity, might, apart from the grace of God, have become comparatively close-handed if she had passed into easy circumstances. Changes scarcely less striking have taken place, for we have seen prosperous men display a lack of liberality, the prediction of which, in the days of their poverty, would have extorted the indignant question, "Is thy servant a dog that he should do this thing?" For the pride and selfishness which prosperity has such power to produce in human hearts, there is one effective preventive or cure—a constant and grateful remembrance of the fact that to God and His goodness all is owing. Nebuchadnezzar looked at the city of palaces in which he reigned, and he cried out, "Is not this great Babylon which I have built?" Then sprang up the pride for which he was so severely punished. Jacob marshalled his flocks and herds and household, and so had all his wealth in sight at one time; but instead of saying, "See what I have gained," he said in spirit, "Behold what God has given me." Then, instead of making him hard-hearted and highminded, his prosperity melted him into tenderness and humbled him to the dust, where he cried, "I am not worthy of the least of all Thy mercies." The arrogance of spirit, and coarseness of speech, and niggardliness of heart, which Nabal displayed, were unmistakeable proofs that in his prosperity he had forgotten the

God to whom he was indebted for it. Hence that which should have made his lowliness to grow and blossom like a lily of the valley, did only serve to make his poisonous pride flourish, like the deadly nightshade, and that which should have filled him with grateful love to God and generous love to men, only helped to increase his self-indulgence and his self-idolatry.

There was another reason why better things might have been reasonably expected of Nabal. God had given him a true help-meet—a woman who, if he had yielded to her influence, would have done much to lift him out of his roughness and wickedness into refinement and godliness. "She was a woman of good understanding and of a beautiful countenance." The companionship of such a one ought to have had some humanising influence upon Nabal, and have saved him at least from the lower depths of folly and brutishness into which he sank. It is one of the marvels of human nature, that some rough and selfish men can live for year after year in fellowship with gentle and self-denying women, and yet be no more impressed and improved by them than the dead heart of Absalom was moved by the tears and wailings of his disconsolate father. You may see a living man living for years with a meek, patient, long-suffering wife, whose love for him nothing can quench, whose devotion to him nothing can impair, and all the while he sinks deeper and deeper into his selfishness and sottishness. There is many a Nabal whose churlishness and godlessness are all the more guilty in the sight of heaven, because of the saintliness of the woman to whom in God's good providence he has been wedded. If such men die impenitent and unpardoned, surely for them condemnation will be heavy and perdition will be deep!

It is time to pass on to the particular circumstances which brought out so fully the worst features in Nabal's character, and aroused so fearfully the resentment of David. Nabal had enough and to spare, while David was in temporary poverty. David was in danger of perishing for lack of a little of that of which Nabal had such an abundance, and therefore the appeal for relief was sent. David seems to have known the kind of man he had to deal with, for he blended prudence with his boldness in begging, and pressed his suit on that day on which above all others it was least likely to fail. Amongst different nations there are different seasons which are specially sacred to hospitality and to generosity. With us in England Christmas has become such a season. Hearts that are flinty at other times are touched into a little feeling then, and fruits of kindness and goodwill are gathered from branches that are barren all the year beside. There are some men whom you would not care to ask for charity at any other season, to whom you would venture to make an appeal if you met them just as Christmas bells were ringing. Amongst the Jews, and other Eastern peoples, the time of sheep-shearing was commonly the season of special liberality; hence, when "David heard in the wilderness that Nabal did shear his sheep," he sent out ten young men to greet him, to express good wishes on his behalf, and to humbly plead for a share of the bounty which it was thought Nabal would be sure to bestow on such an occasion. Beside the force of good old customs, there was another reason why on that particular day David's solicitation was seasonable. It was partly on the ground that his men had been guardians of the flocks that David rested his appeal, and there could not be a better time for that appeal than the season when the flocks were counted and the fleeces were gathered. In order to move Nabal, the messengers were charged to make mention of the timeliness of their visit:—"Thus shall ye say to him that liveth in prosperity, Let the young men find favour in thine eyes, *for we come in a good day.*"

Many have thought that the prudence and policy of David's conduct were more obvious than its dignity. Did he not in some measure demean himself, they ask, by setting forth so fully the services he had rendered? It is not usual, they say, to do a man a good turn, and then to go and tell him all about it, and ask for some grateful recognition of it. Before we blame David for being undignified, let us try to realize his position and his temptations. He must have been in great straits, or he would never have sent in such a way to a man like Nabal. Hunger is a sharp thorn, and impels many a man to do what is far easier for well-fed people to blame than for him to avoid. We are often angry with some of the poor for being mean-spirited and deficient in frankness and straightforwardness. Instead of spending our breath in censuring them, it would sometimes be much better to spend it in thanksgiving that we have not known the special temptations of poverty, and have been placed by a benignant Providence in circumstances wherein it is a comparatively easy thing to maintain "our dignity and independence."

There are people whom you cannot fully know until you ask them for something. While no direct appeal is made to their supposed benevolence, their real character is masked; but the moment you press them to be generous, despite all their efforts to wear it still, the covering drops off, and they stand forth in all their native unsightliness. To what a revelation of Nabal's heart the prayer of David led! How thoroughly the churl disclosed himself, and showed that by the hands of sin the last lingering trace of the image of God's love had been swept from his soul! And yet he tried to cloak his selfishness and justify his meanness by blackening David's character. "Who is David? Who is the son of Jesse? There be many servants now-a-days that break away every man from his master; shall I then take my bread and my water, and my flesh that I have killed for my shearers, and give it unto men whom I know not whence they be?" Nabal could not say it was the wrong day for charity, so he said this was a wrong case. Such people are never destitute of reasons for not giving, and are not ashamed to try and cover their niggardliness with excuses so flimsy that even the sight of a bat would be strong enough to pierce them. To spare their purse they can always find some flaw in the "case," or, failing that, some fault in the applicants who represent the "case," or something unseasonable in the time of making the application. There never yet was an appeal to human kindness which Nabal would not have had some reason for resisting. If he had been placed in circumstances like Abraham, and angels had come to partake of his hospitality, he would probably have cried out, "Give my bread and flesh to people with wings! What next, I wonder!".

The provocation to David must have been great, and we are more grieved than surprised that at once his soul was all on fire with wrath, and he took a solemn oath to destroy Nabal and his men too before the next morning should dawn. David forgot how much God had done for Nabal, what ingratitude God had received at Nabal's hand, and yet how patiently God had borne with him for many years, and how lavishly God had blessed him despite all his guiltiness. We might have hoped that, instead of fostering human vengeance, David would have striven to imitate Divine long-suffering; but the wisest men are not always wise, and the best men are not always consistent. "Wherefore let him that thinketh he standeth, take heed lest he fall." David's lapse was not long lasting; for before he could carry out his angry purpose, his spirit was calmed and his footsteps were checked, and he put his cause into infinitely better keeping than his own. Blessed by God with preventing grace, he acted according to the counsel of his own song:—"Fret not thyself because of evil doers. Rest in the Lord and wait patiently for Him."

The history shows, what is very credible, that Nabal was a great coward as well as a coarse blusterer. When he heard of David's indignation, "his heart died within him, and he became as a stone." It would seem as if the weight of his own craven fears helped to sink him into the grave. Possibly his own cowardice was the instrument with which the Lord smote him; and the terrors of his guilty spirit were the disease of which he died. This much is certain, he perished for his sins. There is no hint that he was indolent or dishonest, and that his wealth had been gained by fraud and falsehood. The head and front of his offending were not seen in the way in which he had secured his prosperity, but in the spirit in which he received and used it. The very day wherein he refused relief to those who had befriended him, "he held a feast in his house like the feast of a king." He had an abundance of this world's goods, and he saw his brother have need, and he shut up his bowels of compassion against him. He is not accused of heresy or idolatry, Sabbath-breaking or blasphemy. He was utterly wanting in meekness and gentleness, courtesy and kindness. He would indulge himself even to gluttony and drunkenness, and yet refused his bread to those who were ready to perish; therefore the anger of the Lord waxed great against him, and swept him into an untimely grave. His name has become imperishable by being written in the book which is to be translated into every tongue and read in every land; but the immortality which Scripture has given him is an immortality of infamy. He has been lifted out of obscurity by the hand of Inspiration; but the elevation given to him is that of the scaffold and the gibbet, on which he is exhibited as a warning to all mankind against those sins of brutish selfishness which are infinitely obnoxious to our Father in heaven, who delighteth in mercy.

V.

DIVINE CORRECTION OF A PROPHET'S MISTAKE, AND DIVINE DENIAL OF A KING'S DESIRE.

———•◦•———

2 SAMUEL vii.

DIVINE CORRECTION OF A PROPHET'S MISTAKE, AND DIVINE DENIAL OF A KING'S DESIRE.

"REMARKABLE answers to prayer" have furnished many with a most encouraging theme. Innumerable instances have been cited wherein blessings, which only the strongest faith would be bold enough to seek, have been secured. Volumes of almost incredible facts have been compiled to show the merciful and marvellous ways in which human desires breathed in supplication are changed into Divine decrees. In many cases it has been proved that while yet the suppliant was on his knees, the Almighty word must have gone forth, "According to thy prayers, so be it unto thee." *Delayed answers to prayer* have not been dealt with so fully and frequently, for they do not constitute a subject so pleasant to our fretful and hurrying nature. They might, however, be oftener discoursed upon with advantage to those (there name is legion) who have not yet learnt how wise it is to "rest in the Lord, and wait patiently for Him." *God's denials of man's requests* are still less frequently the theme of sermon and treatise. They have an appearance of contradicting the promises, and proving that prayer is in vain; and, therefore, perhaps, they are often excluded from purely human histories. With its usual fearlessness and fidelity the Bible records them, and thereby helps us to realise that it cannot always be according to our minds. Apparently sanctified human wills have had to be thwarted by the Divine will; and to what looked like wise and lawful petitions, the answer of Heaven has been an emphatic negative. Moses was mighty in supplication, and more than once his intercession came between the Jewish people and their merited destruction; but his own death in the wilderness was in perfect opposition to his own ardent desires expressed in prayer and enforced by tears. The Apostle Paul had to tell of a thrice-repeated application which met with a thrice-repeated denial. David never prayed more fervently than when he prayed for the life of his child, but he prayed in vain. To human judgment nothing could be more laudable and consistent than his desire to crown the labours of his life by building a temple for the praise and glory of God; and yet, though the king after God's own heart cherished the purpose, and the prophet of the Lord instantly and heartily approved of it, the Divine will was against it, and it had to be relinquished. It might be more pleasant to study the instances in which, through the goodness of God, the desires of David's heart were granted, and his hopes were realised; but it ought to be as profitable to look occasionally at the other side of his experience. God's thoughts are not always our thoughts; and when they differ, ours must give way, and His must prevail. The history now before us shows us that one of God's most faithful and favoured servants had personal experience of this necessity. As we behold David's submission to denial and disappointment, our own ought to become more contented and cheerful.

It is pleasant to glance at the circumstances which gave birth to David's desire to build the Temple. The regal position into which he passed on the death of Saul was no bed of roses. The land was still overrun by the Philistines, who held many of its strongest fortresses. Jerusalem was in the hands of the Jebusites; the people had been crushed by bondage, and impoverished by repeated invasions; the surviving members of the house of Saul, with their partisans, resisted David's claims; and the entire kingdom was in a state of ruin and chaos, which, to the most sanguine, must have made the thought of order and prosperity a forlorn hope. There was hard and long-lasting work to be done, but David gave himself to it with full purpose of heart; and his God who had called him to it did not suffer him to labour in vain. Victory after victory crowned his arduous struggles, until, at last, the Philistines were for ever banished; the Land of Promise was fully possessed by the Israelites; and David's unresisted rule extended over all the twelve tribes. It was a happy time for the King and his people. Those who for years had been forced to struggle for life and liberty could now let the sword rest in its scabbard; instead of the spear they could use the ploughshare, and till the long-neglected fields, and grow the golden harvest, without any fear that ruthless invaders would trample it into the dust or carry it away as spoil. Peace had come into the land, and prosperity was in her train. "THE KING SAT IN HIS HOUSE, AND THE LORD HAD GIVEN HIM REST ROUND ABOUT FROM ALL HIS ENEMIES."

We can scarcely enter into the joy which all this created, and the thankfulness it inspired; not because we know nothing of such circumstances, but because we have always lived in them. Those who have never mourned on account of the deep darkness of midnight, cannot appreciate the beauty of the dawn and the splendours of the noon like men who through long hours of thick gloom have watched and waited for the morning. How can we estimate the blessedness of peace and security, as it was estimated by the Hebrews after nearly a life-time of constant disquiet and bloody strife, and well-grounded dread of national annihilation and of individual slavery or death? The sight of his own and his people's prosperity and freedom touched the spirit of David with mighty power, and made it to glow with unwonted gratitude; and he longed to do some great thing to show the love of which his heart was so full: "What shall I render unto the Lord for all His benefits toward me?"

It may be asked, If David were so joyous and thankful, could he not have taken his harp of sweet and solemn sound, and have expressed his new-born praise in some new-born psalm? Doubtless he did this, but it was not enough to satisfy his gratitude. The truly thankful heart is glad to put on its singing robes, and lift its exultant strains to heaven; but it cannot be contented with words and music alone, even though another David should pen the hymn, and an inspired Handel should compose the melody. It will want to express its emotion in works, to put on the garb of a willing servant, and, in addition to saying great things about God, to do right and good and noble things for God. In the matter of word-praise, David possessed a power and reached a position absolutely unrivalled; but, perfect as he could make the service of song, that did not suffice for him when God was crowning his life with such loving-kindness and tender mercies. Let us be assured that if 'we know and believe the love that God hath to us,"—if His love have enkindled ours,—we too shall be eager to embody our living thankfulness in deeds of truth, and kindness, and purity. The praise that expresses itself in action is not only the most acceptable to God, it is also the only praise which can give relief to the spirit burdened with a sense of what it owes to Him, whose mercy is like Himself—without beginning of days or end of years.

The ark of the covenant was still kept in the tabernacle—a structure which had been intended for the sacred services of the tribes in the days of their pilgrimage only. The King felt that while it might have been pardonable to retain this temporary house of prayer during the time the people were in an unsettled political and social condition, it would not be seemly to continue it when their own dwellings were of a more costly and durable character, and their full and peaceful establishment in the Promised Land was through the goodness of their God accomplished. He, therefore, formed the purpose of building an enduring temple in the place of the frail tent, hoping that he might thereby appropriately show his own thankfulness, and make the provision for the national worship to be more in accordance with the national prosperity. David knew by experience that acceptable worship could be rendered apart from all costly or consecrated structures, for he had himself sung God's praises and secured His blessing in wilderness places, and in dens and caves of the earth. What was afterwards said of his Son and Lord could have been said of him also—

> "Cold mountains and the midnight air
> Witnessed the fervour of His prayer."

At the same time he had a conscientious conviction that the externals of a people's worship ought to be in keeping with the externals of their secular life. It shocked his sense of consistency when he realised the fact that he dwelt in a house of cedar, while the ark of God dwelt in curtains. The principle which David recognised was one which in after-days the prophets enforced upon the people by Divine command—"Is it time for you, O ye, to dwell in your ceiled houses, and this house lie waste?" Spirituality of worship is the great essential, and God can be served acceptably in the meanest structure; but it would not look well for people to live in palaces and worship in barns. There would be at least an appearance of evil, if nothing but poor and shabby sanctuaries could be found in the streets wherein the bank and the exchange, and even the warehouses, are massive and costly buildings. A stranger would suppose that he had come amongst a people who were starving their religion, while they were pampering everything else belonging to them.

We must turn from the origin and nature of David's purpose to Nathan's mistaken sanction of it. A sympathetic heart is a great quickener of the brain. If your spirit be in unison with that of another man, how readily you and he can understand each other. Half words are enough, and either of you can fully discern the other's desire or purpose long before his language has fully disclosed it. . It is this law of our nature which makes it so much easier for a man to find out the Divine will when his heart is brought into living sympathy with God. Then his faculty of discernment is so perfect, that to him God can say, "I will guide thee with Mine eye." Between Nathan and David there was this sympathy, so that the latter had scarcely begun to speak about his purpose before the former divined all that he intended. "The King said to the prophet, See now, I dwell in a house of cedar, but the ark of God dwelleth within curtains. And the prophet said to the King, Go, do all that is in thine heart: for the Lord is with thee." The thing seemed so obviously right and good to Nathan, that he did not wait to give it further consideration; and instead of saying, "I will pray about it, and seek to learn the will of God concerning it," he ventured at once to promise Divine approval and blessing of it. He thought he had "the mind of the Spirit," and mistook the promptings of his own heart for a voice from heaven. Here is a most instructive case of the fallibility of an always good and ofttimes inspired man! It is frequently difficult to distinguish between the inclinations of our own wills and the guidance of God's hand. It is so easy to mistake the bent of our own desires for the intimations of Providence; and when our own hearts are in favour of a thing it requires little argument to convince us that God is in favour of it too. No matter how wise or right any course may appear to be, if we would be always safe we must always distrust our own unaided judgments, and cherish the dependent and teachable spirit which cries, "Lord, what wilt Thou have me to do?"

Nathan went home to his evening prayer, and his nightly rest, and was speedily made aware of his error. "*It came to pass that night, that the Word of the Lord came unto Nathan, saying, Go and tell my servant David, Thus saith the Lord. Thou shalt not build Me a house for Me to dwell in.*" In after-days, Nathan was sent of God to rebuke David for his sin; and he went to the offending monarch with a holy courage and fidelity which did him honour. Now he was sent on what was a very different, and in some respects a more difficult errand; not to chide David for a fault, but to recall his own words, and to confess that he had spoken as in God's name, when he had not God's authority for what he said.

Many have written in glorious strains of Nathan's rebuke of David. His wisdom was as great as his fearlessness. What point and power in the parable whereby he got the royal sinner to unwittingly sit in judgment on himself! What noble forgetfulness of everything but his duty in that home-thrust, "Thou art the man!" How it pierced the callousness of David's spirit, awoke his sleeping conscience, and made his hitherto impenitent heart to bleed with a godly anguish! Still, one has often thought, that if he had the artistic skill to paint a gallery of Scripture portraits, and if he were to delineate that one scene in each man's life in which he most displayed the beauty and glory of his saintliness, he would depict Nathan in the presence of the King, not when he said to David, "Thou hast sinned," but when he said, "I spoke in haste yesterday; I had no warrant for saying that the Lord would be with thee in this purpose. He has shown me my mistake, and I am come to confess and to correct it." Who does not know that to take even a mote out of his own eye is a greater proof of saintly skill than to help to take a beam out of another's eye? Are not the words, "I was wrong," three of the hardest in the language for any one to utter?

Most of us might live for centuries, and never have an opportunity of imitating the fearlessness of Nathan in telling a king of his sins. None of us can live for many years, without having frequent opportunities of imitating Nathan in the frankness with which he acknowledged his error and his fault as soon as he was made conscious of them. "Confess your faults one to another," is a Divine injunction, and it would not be easy to exaggerate the mischief which arises from our disobedience to it. Hearts that once seemed inseparably bound together are estranged and made the seat of dislike; men who once helped each other, now stand aloof in mutual coldness and hurtfulness; families are rent asunder, and churches are enfeebled, because those who have been foolish or faulty have not the manliness to avow it, and to seek the forgiveness which confession is so certain to secure. In both secular and spiritual communities, unconfessed faults are like thorns which are left in the flesh; they have pierced till the wound festers, and the blood becomes feverish, and foul disease threatens to spread over the whole body. All honour to the man who, when he has blundered or sinned, will honestly acknowledge it with becoming sorrow! The curse of the offender may have rested on him for a while, but the blessing of the peacemaker shall be finally his. God be praised for the grace of confession which He gives to His guilty children! It is the sign of returning wisdom. It is the precursor of pardon, and the pledge of reformation. It is often the dawn of an everlasting day.

We have now to look at the denial of David's desire, and at the facts and promises which were set before him to reconcile him to his disappointment. There was neither disdain of his gratitude nor condemnation of his idea that the prospered nation ought to have a better house for holy service. The Lord in His great kindness was careful so to convey the denial that it could not possibly impair David's faith in the Divine love, nor excite his hostility to the Divine plan. He testified that God's gentleness had made him great. Of that gentleness he seldom had richer experience than on this occasion. The Lord might have set forth His sovereignty, and have said, "It is My will that you should not do this work. To My decision you must submit without any explanations on My part, and without any questioning on yours. Have I not a right to do as I please, without trying to justify My ways to any of My servants?" Not as a king with his servants, but as a father with his children, the God of David acted. Never did a compassionate father display a deeper anxiety to retain his child's confidence, and comfort his child's heart, while for wise reasons he was compelled to thwart his child's purpose! The faith of His children in His wisdom and love, and their cheerful submission to His will, are pleasant things in the sight of the Lord; and therefore He does not simply command and forbid, but He reasons with us and explains to us, and is far more anxious to prove His kindness than to assert His authority. Lord, what is man's confidence in Thee, that Thou shouldst take such pains to secure it? Thou hast magnified him, and set Thine heart upon him!

The first words in the message were calculated to pacify David's conscience, which had been troubled about the poverty of the place wherein God was worshipped. He was reminded that the matter which had distressed him had called forth no complaint from the Lord. "*Whereas I have not dwelt in any house since the time that I brought up the children of Israel out of Egypt, even to this day, but have walked in a tent and in a tabernacle. In all the places wherein I have walked with all the children of Israel, spake I a word with any of the tribes of Israel—saying, Why build ye not Me an house of Cedar?*" For four hundred years the people had been in Canaan, and during those centuries the tabernacle had been the only house of God in the land. But He had never once chided any of the rulers of the nation for this. Was that long silence a sign of His indifference as to the way in which the people worshipped Him? There are facts which forbid us to put this interpretation upon it. Was it not rather a sign of His forbearance, and of His consideration of the people's circumstances? He knew their troubled state, the peril they were in because of their implacable enemies, and what hard work it was for them to hold the land and maintain their own freedom! It was true that their sins had been the great source of their difficulties, but still the Lord did not forget those difficulties; and when His people were struggling with them, He was neither rigorous in His demands, nor severe in His judgments. He pitied where He might have chided, and maintained a charitable silence when He might have uttered righteous and indignant complaints. Some one may ask, "What had this past forbearance toward those who had not built a better sanctuary, to do with the present denial of him who wished to raise a fitting house for the Lord?" It showed that in relation to this matter of tabernacle and temple, the course pursued by God for many generations had been one of gentleness and grace. Would not that help David to believe that God's present and future course, in relation to the same matter, would be marked by the same characteristics? Whatever testified to the Lord's kindness would promote David's hearty acquiescence in His dealings. Single events in the providence of God must not be isolated and then judged. They must be looked at in the light of what (without irreverence) we may call the established character of Him who worketh all things according to the counsel of His will.

Having referred to the forbearance which others had met with, the Divine message proceeds to speak of what had been done for David. "*Now therefore so shalt thou say unto My servant David,*

Thus saith the Lord of hosts, I took thee from the sheepcote, from following the sheep, to be ruler over My people, over Israel: And I was with thee whithersoever thou wentest, and have cut off all thine enemies out of thy sight, and have made thee a great name, like unto the name of the great men that are in the earth." The Lord spake as if He feared that by thwarting David's purpose He might expose His love to unjust suspicion; and therefore He was careful to show that He had already done so much for His servant, that, whatever course He might see it best to pursue, His love ought not to be suspected for a moment. Surely He had placed that beyond the shadow of a doubt! "I am about to say thee nay," He said, "but let not My refusal provoke thy mistrust. When thou art thinking of what I deny thee, think also of what I have given thee. I found thee in obscurity, and I have lifted thee to fame. I found thee in the sheepfold, and I have lifted thee to the throne. I found thee in peril and in poverty and in shame, and I have placed thee in safety; I have surrounded thee with wealth, I have enshrined thee in glory. In a thousand ways I have proved to thee that I have loved thee with an unfailing love. However much of supposed good I may withhold from thee,—however much of real disappointment I may lay upon thee,—no misgiving as to my love should trouble thee and dishonour Me. After such an experience as thou hast had, thou oughtest to be able to say in all things, 'It is the Lord! He cannot be unkind to me! It is the same loving-kindness always, though sometimes it forbids my desire and rejects my supplication.'" The way in which David's doubts were prevented is the way in which ours must be checked and cured. If God's nay to our requests should tempt us to distrust His love, we must meet the temptation with memories of the many times and the manifold ways wherein He has heard our prayer and enriched us with His blessing. Discontented brooding over the few and the little things denied, must be supplanted by grateful meditation on the many and great things bestowed. We must not be beguiled by that craft of the wicked one which seduced the mother of us all into dissatisfaction and disobedience. If the tempter begin to talk to us about the one tree whose fruit we must not gather, be it ours to speak instantly about the thousand trees of whose fruit we may freely eat. If the Lord were to speak of all that He has done for us and given to us, He might tell a more wondrous story of His love than that in which the elevation and enthronement of David were described. He that spared not His own Son, but delivered Him up for us all, how can He fail in kindness to us? If He were to reject our petitions and thwart our desires a thousand times, our faith, sustained by experience, ought to rise above all denial and disappointment. After what we have seen of His grace in the Gospel, it is reason, as well as faith, for each one of us to say, "Though He slay me, yet will I trust in Him."

There is great significance in the fact that in

refusing David the coveted honour of building the temple, the Lord reminded him of the glory as well as the mercy already bestowed upon him: "*I have made thee a great name, like unto the names of the great ones that are in the earth.*" Was it not telling David that the fame he had secured was enough for any one man's lawful ambition? To him had been given the honour of rising to regal dignity, of delivering the nation from the danger and degradation which had lasted for generations, of reducing a chaotic kingdom to order, and of producing prosperity unheard of before. Why should he want to add to that the glory of being the greatest temple-builder the world had seen? He must not aspire to that crown too. God would reserve it for another; for it is not His pleasure that all the brilliancy of great achievements shall belong to only one name, and that all the joy of great successes shall flood only one heart. Excepting the kingdom of God's grace, there are to be no more world-wide monarchies. There must be sceptres for many hands and crowns for many heads, for the Lord will not favour the monopolising spirit. The old motto, "*Live and let live,*" is unspeakably more in accordance with His will than the modern notion of one man grasping at well-nigh everything. Covetous men may not put any limit to their desires, but God will put limits to their powers. This is a great good; for if some men had opportunities and faculties equal to their ambition, all the business of the city would be absorbed into two or three establishments, and all the ships in the docks would belong to two or three firms, and all the great profits of commerce would be swept into two or three coffers. Men righteously denounced Napoleon for his desire to make a French empire of all Europe. There is too often a Napoleonism in commerce which is not a whit more admirable. Instead of vigorously and contentedly pursuing their own proper business, men have sought profitable pecuniary connection with ten or twenty other totally distinct enterprises. In how many cases this vaulting ambition has overleaped itself! How much of present depression and difficulty has come from practical forgetfulness of the obvious truth, that it is not God's will that a few men should have everything, but that honours, and profits, and pleasures should be widely distributed! Men may determine "to have many irons in the fire," but God will not give them hands enough to handle them all skilfully; and, therefore, sooner or later, fingers are sure to be burnt. In moralising upon this matter, we have travelled further than we intended from things ecclesiastical into things secular; but it is easy to return by simply remarking, that the spirit we have tried to describe and deprecate sometimes creeps into the Church, where it is more unseemly and reprehensible than in the world.

From another part of the inspired history we learn that the character of David's preceding work was given as one reason why the present purpose was to be laid aside: "*But God said, Thou shalt not build an house for my name, because thou hast been a man of war, and hast shed blood."** It should not be supposed that this implies censure of David's warlike course. Had he not been qualified for it, and called to it, by God? Was it not a necessary work, and had he not Divine succour in it? It was both lawful and expedient; and yet it had unfitted him for the new kind of work to which he wanted to put his hands. In our present imperfect state, ability for one thing may involve disability for another thing. As no one man is intended to gain everything, so no one man is endowed with all the talents. Happy is he who finds out what he is fit for, and devotes himself to it; and is either so wise or so busy that he does not attempt numerous other achievements. It is too often assumed that because a man is gifted for "the work of the ministry," he is equally gifted for many other things. He is expected to be an "Admirable Crichton," to whom a scientific lecture, a literary essay, a political oration, a secretary's duties, and the labours of a

* 1 Chron. xxviii. 3.

counsellor to all classes on all subjects, are as congenial as the preaching of a sermon, and none of them

> " more difficile
> Than for a blackbird 'tis to whistle."

If he fought battles as successfully as David, some people would be surprised if he could not also build temples as magnificently as Solomon. The alleged author of "Ecce Homo" has well said, that in these days of varied demands and multiplied endeavours, one of the first conditions of ministerial success is that the minister impress himself with the fact that he has not the genius for doing everything. We should learn this lesson for the times from the life of David, that great success in one department of labour may actually disqualify a man for another department. Not because he had been such a bad warrior, but because he had been such a good one, David was to leave temple-building for another to undertake.

Another way in which the Lord sought to reconcile David to the denial of his desire, was by promising that his purpose should not perish, but be carried out by his own son. *"And when the days be fulfilled, I will set up thy seed after thee, and I will establish his kingdom. He shall build an house for my name, and I will establish the throne of his kingdom for ever."* It is no wonder that God's message checked all murmuring and rebellion in David's heart. He did more than cheerfully submit; he exulted in the decision and purpose of the Lord. Instead of weeping and wailing, because his plan had not been adopted, he broke out into an impassioned and sublime strain of thanksgiving. He looked at the greatness and glory God had promised to his house; and as he gazed at that, he could no more see the denial of his request, than he could have seen the faintest of the far-off stars while he was looking at the lustre of the noon-tide sun. With thoughts of mercies past and mercies to come filling his mind, there was no room for discontent on account of present disappointment. Let it be remembered to the honour of his piety, that such was his confidence in the wisdom and love and faithfulness of God, that one of the most fervent songs he ever sung was inspired by the very message in which he was told he was not to do what he had asked to do. "THEN WENT KING DAVID IN AND SAT BEFORE THE LORD AND SAID, WHO AM I, O LORD GOD, AND WHAT IS MY HOUSE, THAT THOU HAST BROUGHT ME HITHERTO? AND THIS WAS YET A SMALL THING IN THY SIGHT, O LORD GOD: BUT THOU HAST SPOKEN ALSO OF THY SERVANT'S HOUSE FOR A GREAT WHILE TO COME. AND IS THIS THE MANNER OF MAN, O LORD GOD? FOR THY WORD'S SAKE, AND ACCORDING TO THINE OWN HEART, HAST THOU DONE ALL THESE GREAT THINGS, TO MAKE THY SERVANT KNOW THEM? WHEREFORE THOU ART GREAT, O LORD GOD; FOR THERE IS NONE LIKE UNTO THEE, NEITHER IS THERE ANY GOD BESIDE THEE."

It ought to be easier for us to imitate David's hearty acquiescence, because we know that subsequent events proved how wise it was. According to God's promise, Solomon succeeded to the throne, and was in every way fitted for the task assigned to him. His reign was one of profound peace and profuse plenty. He was inspired with loftiest ideas of magnificence, and, having treasure and skill at his command, his hands could achieve what his thoughts dictated. Into the work of building the temple he was able to press not only the zeal of the Jews, but also the enterprise and genius of the Gentiles. The sacred structure was completed according to a scale of grandeur far exceeding any conceptions which the Psalmist had formed. As it stood there in all its splendour, vocal with Divine praises and filled with Divine glory, who could doubt that the Lord had done right in deciding (against the prayer of His servant) that not David but Solomon should build it? It was a magnificent testimony to the truth that God's "Nay" and God's "Yea" are only two different forms in which the same everlasting love and infinite wisdom are expressed.

VI.

GREAT TROUBLES FOLLOWING GREAT TRANSGRESSIONS.

———◆◆◆———

Proverbs xiv. 14.

"The backslider in heart shall be filled with his own ways; and a good man shall be satisfied from himself."

GREAT TROUBLES FOLLOWING GREAT TRANSGRESSIONS.

IF Solomon had been asked for practical confirmation of these words, he could have replied, that proofs of both statements were to be found in the history of one and the same man. When he drew the sharp contrast, he might have been thinking of two totally different sides of his own father's experience. David reveals himself to us in the Psalms in the most unreserved manner, and the revelation shows us that his godliness was a well-spring of delight in his heart. A bad man's belief in the existence of God is a trouble and a torment to him. It is a fruitful root of fear and disquiet in his soul, which he would pluck up, if his instincts and reason did not prevent him. A good man's belief in God is a fountain of peace and joy and hope. It furnishes wings to his spirit, wherewith he can rise at will into those higher regions which clouds never darken, and tempests never disturb. As a good man, David found his belief in the Supreme One to be an unfailing help and comfort. His gratitude, his obedience, his confidence, his love, and all the other goodly graces of his soul, were a cause of intense present delight, as well as a prophecy of future perfection and glory. He had not to be always searching for sources of pleasure outside of himself. When every external stream was dried up, he could retire within himself, and drink of the fountain which the Spirit of God had created there. Because he was "a good man," he was "satisfied from himself."

But David became a backslider, and then there followed a long and sad experience which fully verified the first part of the proverb. Men sometimes speak, not of David's great *sins*, but of his great *sin*, as if he were guilty of only one flagrant transgression. Such language is lenient at the expense of truth. A great sin seldom stands altogether alone. It is most frequently found in the midst of kindred company, like a high Alpine peak—a region of desolation and death, surrounded by other desolate peaks only a little lower than itself. In David's case it was not one monster transgression, but several which lifted themselves in colossal defiance of God's law. For the concealment of one sin others were necessary; and what aggravated the guiltiness was the fact, that, while the first sin was probably unpremeditated, the other offences were certainly wrought deliberately, and with deep design. The offender against man and God might plead, that at first he was swept into transgression by a sudden gust of passion; but he could not urge any such extenuation of his sins when he tempted Uriah to drunkenness; when he sent the patriotic soldier back to the camp with a letter containing a plan whereby his fidelity and courage might be taken advantage of to accomplish his destruction; and when he used his kingly power in commanding Joab to help him in this murderous policy. There are few things in history more appalling than the the awful completeness of David's transgressions. His offences lacked little or nothing to perfect their rankness, and make them "smell to heaven." Having brought himself into difficulties by his crime, he grappled with the difficulties with a masterful energy and a terrible recklessness, as if he would shrink from nothing, and spare nobody, in his endeavour to hide his own shame. The ravages made by sin in his nature, in a short season, were incredibly great. Who could have supposed that such selfishness, and meanness, and hypocrisy, were possible in one who for years had proved himself to be so generous, and noble, and real? How utterly unlike himself David was, when he tried to cover his delight at Uriah's death with canting words about the chances of war and the duty of resignation! What a pitiable pretence it was to send a message to Joab, exhorting him not to be too much distressed and discouraged by the calamity which had befallen the army: "*Thus shalt thou say unto Joab, Let not this thing displease thee, for the sword devoureth one as well as another; make thy battle more strong against the city and overthrow it; and encourage thou him.*" First, a secret letter to Joab, in which it was written: "Set ye Uriah in the fore-front of the hottest battle, and retire ye from him that he may die;" and next a public message to comfort the commander under the bereavement he had sustained! Can this be David? Is this what sin does with a man when he suffers it to have place and power in his heart? The sight of such havoc wrought in one who was a king amongst the great and good, might well dim the brightness and disturb the joy of heaven itself. It ought to have been sufficient to make the Tempter and Destroyer of men weep over the ruin he had accomplished. It has made strong ones tremble and brave ones quail, and in hearts innumerable it has intensified the yearning after the better country where, to saved and sheltered human nature, such sin and such damage are impossible.

Our present object is not to set forth either the repentance or the forgiveness of David, but to show that, though he was penitent and pardoned, he sustained great loss and damage by reason of his sins. A later psalmist, in describing God's dealings with the Jews, states that both pardon and punishment were dealt out to them. "*Thou wast a God that forgavest them, though Thou tookest vengeance of their inventions.*"* This blending of mercy and judgment, forgiveness and chastisement, may seem contradictory, if not impossible, to those who make the always harmful and often fatal mistake of taking one-sided views of the Divine character and government; but the history of the Church abounds with illustrations of it. The mercy which forgave, and restored, and

---

* Psalm xcix. 8.—In the English edition of Hengstenberg on the Psalms, the passage is rendered as follows: "Thou wast a forgiving God to them, and an avenging God because of their iniquities."

cleansed David, did not stay all the evil consequences of his transgressions, but left the backslider to eat much of the bitter fruit of his ways.

Punishment for his sin preceded his penitence and forgiveness. For a whole year David remained in that strangest greatest guilt of all— an unconsciousness of guilt. We do not know with what opiates he drugged his conscience; but how fast asleep it was we learn from the trouble Nathan had to arouse it. How blind he must have been, not to have instantly discerned an image of himself in the mirror the prophet held up before him! His spiritual sensibilities were so deadened he did not imagine there was any reference to him in the story Nathan told. There is no evidence that he would have dreamed of applying it to himself, if the prophet had not said, "*Thou art the man.*" If his conscience had been tender and wakeful, he would have caught Nathan's meaning before the story was half told, and he would have thought that men were referring to his fall when they had no intention of alluding to it. With great beams in both his own eyes, he was yet determined to put another man to death for having a mote in one of his. This long-lasting and deep forgetfulness of his own state is one of the most fearful things belonging to David's declension. The sin which makes it so important and necessary for a man to know himself, is the very thing which most robs him of the power of knowing himself. Who can understand his errors? While David was forgetting his transgressions, God was setting them in the light of His countenance—the light that most reveals the infulsness of sin. Describing that period of his impenitence, David says, "*My bones waxed old through my roaring all the day long. For day and night Thy hand was heavy upon me; my moisture is turned into the drought of summer.*" Some have supposed that these words refer to a punishment actually inflicted upon David in the form of a bodily sickness. This is very possible, for sickness of the body is one of the messengers God sends to bring the sins of the soul to mind. Burning fever or wasting consumption has strange power to quicken dead consciences and to awaken sleeping memories. Many an old man has been made "to possess the sins of his youth" by the instrumentality of some bodily affliction. It may be that in some such way David was made to suffer before he repented. Others suppose that the words quoted above refer only to a dread of punishment which David had prior to his forgiveness. This is quite compatible with the fact, that he failed to confess his sins, and even forgot their heinousness. Apart from deep conviction of guilt, there might have been a vague apprehension of coming evil, disturbing his peace, and devouring his strength. Whether it were disease of body, or melancholy of mind, it was from the hand of the Lord, and it was because of his unforgiven and unconfessed transgressions.

When at length David acknowledged his sins, and cried for mercy, he was met by God with wondrous grace. The promptness of the pardon proves that God does, indeed, delight in mercy. As in the case of the returning prodigal, David was scarcely allowed to finish his confession, before the prophet exclaimed: "*The Lord also hath put away thy sin; thou shalt not die.*" The words of forgiveness were, however, coupled with a prophecy of woe which was soon fulfilled: "*The child that is born unto thee shall surely die.*" The sight of the stricken child vainly struggling for life, must have pierced the heart of David as with a two-edged sword. If a father have any fragment of a man's heart left in him, he must be crushed by the spectacle of his own children bearing a heavy part of the curse of his own sins. That spectacle has often moved the most hardened men to tears, and the dread of beholding it has been one of the shields which good men have lifted between themselves and temptation. What inexpressible agony David must have endured, as he looked at the innocent sufferer, and said, "It is because of my sin that this little one has been racked with pain and devoured by disease!" With what earnestness and holy indignation he would have repudiated the lie, if any fanatic had gone to him then, saying, "God does not punish sin in His chosen ones!" With what horror he would have repelled the temptation, if any mercy-abusing Antinomian had whispered in his ear, "Let us continue in sin, for grace doth abound!" "Nay," he would have answered, "let us rather shun the very appearance of evil. Grace does abound. Mercy is granted, but still my wickedness corrects me; my backslidings reprove me; I am learning with fresh force that it is an evil and a bitter thing to forsake the Lord!"

What we say of fire or water might have been truly said of Joab, David's commander-in-chief. He was a good servant, but a bad master. One of the evil results of the sins in the matter of Uriah was, that it changed the position of Joab. Henceforth he was more like David's master than David's servant. For the sake of his dignity and honour and peace it was of first importance that the King should have full control over his impulsive and unscrupulous general;

but how could he retain that control after the scene in front of the walls of Rabbah? From the moment that fatal letter was put into Joab's hand, he must have felt that David was utterly in his power. What a secret for a servant to possess concerning his master! There are facts which give us glimpses of the way Joab used the power he had acquired. It was he who thrust the rebel Absalom through with darts, despite the King's explicit command that the traitor should not be slain in his sins. This showed how he set himself above David's authority. There was much wisdom in the rebuke he administered to David about his excessive grief over Absalom's death, but the insolent manner in which he administered it was another proof that the nominal servant had become the real master. When David promoted Amasa, Joab showed his respect for the King's will by deliberately assassinating the man the king delighted to honour. On his death-bed, David revealed the soreness of heart which the tyranny and disobedience and defiance of Joab had caused him; and he besought Solomon to inflict the punishment which he himself had been unable to inflict. This is one of the curses which follow sin; it puts the sinner into the power of other men, and they often use the power to drive him into further sin. Pilate longed to set Jesus free, but he dared not do it for fear of the priests and Pharisees. It was his former misdeeds which had robbed the Roman governor of his power, and made him that day—to a great extent—the mere creature of the envious and murderous foes of the Son of man. If we would maintain our fearlessness and freedom, we must maintain our consistency and purity. As surely as any man flagrantly violates truth and righteousness, so surely he puts himself into the clutches of somebody, whose grip will be neither pleasant nor helpful to him.

A proper control over Joab could not have been the only power David lost through his sins. The power of rebuke was most essential to him.

As a father, how much need there was for him to use it amongst his own sinful children! As a king, how much need for him to use it over his subjects; and, as a prophet, what need for him to use it in the Church! But, when he sinned so fearfully, he must have sinned away well-nigh all his force for rebuking others. That power in his hands could never have been the same after his fall as it had been before. As in former times, men's transgressions might make rivers of water run down his eyes, but how could he severely chide the wrong-doers? If he had begun to speak sternly, he would have been instantly met with a look which would have plainly said, "Physician, heal thyself! Backslider, think of thine own sins!" He had to go softly all the rest of his days. He might declare the tender mercies of the Lord, but he could not, as he used to do, speak of the judgments of God and make his words a perfect terror to evil-doers. Doubtless there were many times when the sight of some flagrant sin enkindled fires of indignation within him, and he was about to speak like a holy prophet of the Lord; but suddenly the memory of his own trespasses slew the unspoken rebuke upon his lips. Imperfect and inconsistent people may proclaim the love of God with fervour; but a man's power to speak of punishment, and to wield the terrors of the Lord effectively, is always proportionate to his personal purity and consistency. David's loss of this power was the loss of so much fitness for saintly service. It was a feebleness which must have been an agony to him whenever he realised it, for nothing but his own sin had caused it. When he saw the force of evil passion in Amnon and Absalom, how he must have hated his own iniquities, if only for this reason, they had crippled the hand wherewith he should have held back his loved ones from the way that leadeth to death!

We learn from several Psalms that David suffered much from slander. He was a successful man, and his success excited envy, and envy gave birth to calumny. Hence we hear him complaining of false accusations, and appealing from the aspersions of men to the judgment of God. It is not possible to fix the dates of all the Psalms in which he refers to these slanders, but we may be sure he was likely to suffer most from this cause after his backslidings. This would be especially true of such calumnies as those of which he complains so piteously in the forty-first Psalm. His great sins must have facilitated the work of the backbiters—for when a man has actually done two or three very evil things, it is easy to get belief for almost any lying story to his detriment. The facts give an air of probability to the falsehoods. The old truths concerning the man are as wings on which the new lies are borne hither and thither and everywhere. This helps to make it so difficult to regain a lost reputation. Long after the man has recovered his moral health, busy tongues will wag against him, and affirm that there are new eruptions of the old disease. It must be hard to bear, but it is one of the evil consequences of sin which we can surely escape only by eschewing all sin. In the day of his adversity David learned fully what men had thought of him in the day of his prosperity. The coarse, cruel, and false things which Shimei said, when he cursed the fugitive King, were said then for the first time to the King's face, but doubtless they had been often said by others behind his back. How much David must have suffered as he saw that it was his own sins which had furnished a basis of truth for this superstructure of calumnies! How he must have then hated his sins, if only for this reason—they had given implements to the hands of the slanderers, with which they might the more readily destroy his reputation, and thereby damage religion and dishonour God! We may not be able to shield ourselves against backbiters, for He who was incarnate perfection did not enjoy that security. This, however, we may do, by the help of God,— so maintain our consistency and integrity, that there shall be no flagrant fault in us to give plausibility to what the poisoned tongue of slander affirms.

A father's happiness is largely in the keeping of his children. If they go wrong, there will be always bitterness in his cup, and a blight upon his joy, notwithstanding any amount of temporal prosperity he may have. If they turn out well, he will find in their good characters a set-off against many calamities, and a region to which his troubled thoughts may often repair for sunshine and solace. As the custodians of their father's happiness, some of David's children proved to be very heartless and faithless. The career of Amnon and Absalom would, under any circumstances, have been sufficient to put a lasting sadness into David's heart. Who then can describe the grief it must have been to him, seeing he was assured that it was to no little extent the fruit of his own evil example and the curse which followed his own sins? It is only as we remember this, that we can fully appreciate his unutterable agony when Absalom perished.

David prayed for pardon, for purity, and for a restoration of spiritual joy. It does not appear that this side the grave he received a large answer to the last request. Traces of the mischief which had been wrought were visible down to the latest hour of life. The splendour of his reputation and the exulting gladness of his spirit were never fully recovered. It was impossible, for, though God had forgiven, David could not forget. The life-long memory of his sins must have been a life-long trouble. The more he realised that God had forgiven him, the less he could forgive himself. It mattered not in what fair scenes and prosperous circumstances he was placed, his thoughts would be travelling back to that dark and doleful region, and fetching thence materials for present gloom and grief.

> "If sad the thought of sweetness gone,
>   If pain past pleasures bring,
> How shall my sins be gazed upon,
>   And not resume their sting?
>
> "Hath not Thy mercy made me whole?
>   Hath not Thy grace forgiven?
> Yet still the grief regains my soul,
>   Yet still my heart is riven.

> "Those buried sins of mine arise,
> Again my heart runs o'er;
> Once more those deep, repentant sighs,
> Those bitter tears once more."

David's experience proves the wisdom of his prayer for preventing grace: "*Keep back Thy servant also from presumptuous sins.*" Prevention *is* better than cure. Prevention is better than pardon. For the son who had never wandered, there could be no such feast of welcome as there was for the returned prodigal; but the father, while justifying the festivities, was careful to protest against the elder brother's notion that the pardoned profligate was having by far the best lot. For him who had not gone away to sow his wild oats and garner the harvest of woe in his heart, there could be no rapturous joy of restoration: but who can tell the greatness of the blessing which belonged to him, even the blessing referred to by his father in those few words of unfathomable meaning: "*Son, thou art ever with me, and all that I have is thine!*"

VII.

THE QUICKENING OF DAVID'S CONSCIENCE BY RIZPAH'S EXAMPLE.

2 SAMUEL xxi. 1—14.

THE QUICKENING OF DAVID'S CONSCIENCE BY RIZPAH'S EXAMPLE.

SOME years since it was found that many returned emigrants were ending their days in English workhouses. When the authorities inquired into the causes of this fact, they ascertained that in nearly every case those who were then paupers had formerly prospered in the colonies; but they had forsaken their prosperity and come back to England, because they could not bear the thought of dying and being buried in the strange lands wherein they had made their homes for a season. While they were in health and vigour, they were comparatively content to be far away from the old country; but as soon as the shadows of evening began to fall, they yearned to return to the familiar haunts of life's morning, in order that, when they fell asleep, they might be laid to rest in their fathers' sepulchres. The desire was so strong, that they yielded to it, although they thereby doomed themselves to poverty for the remainder of their days. This is an instinct which cannot be put down by force of argument. After all that can be said about the unwisdom of it, the voice of nature will still plead for it, and "it seems to be the appointment of heaven that the first attachments of which the heart is conscious should be its last." If we have no such desire about our own final resting-places, we have about those of our friends, and we like to have the graves of our loved ones near to us, and not far away amongst strangers.

> " 'Tis well; 'tis something; we may stand
>   Where he in English earth is laid,
>   And from his ashes may be made
> The violet of his native land.

> "'Tis little; but it looks in truth
> As if the quiet bones were blest,
> Among familiar names to rest
> And in the places of his youth."

This feeling must not be denounced as mere sentimentalism, for it has been cherished as an honourable thing by men who were neither feeble nor foolish. It prevailed amongst the Jews in ancient days, and strong and sainted men were not ashamed to own it. When Barzillai pleaded against the preferment which David was urging upon him, this was his last and most forcible entreaty:—"*Let thy servant, I pray thee, turn back again; that I may die in mine own city, and be buried by the grave of my father and my mother.*" David must have been aware of the prevalence and power of this feeling amongst his fellow-Israelites, and there can be little doubt that he fully sympathised with it. Was it not strange that he should for so many years leave the remains of Saul and Jonathan in the place of their hasty sepulture, far from the burial place of their fathers? When the King and his sons fell in the field of Gilboa, the Philistines exulted with a cruel and savage exultation, and did their utmost to dishonour the dead. They carried the armour of the slain into the house of their god, and the bodies of the monarch and the princes they ignominiously affixed to the wall of a city near to the battle-field. In the first days of his sovereignty Saul had rendered great service to the people of Jabesh-Gilead, and his good deed was not forgotten after his death. The men of that city heard of the indignity done to the dead, and they braved many dangers in a successful effort to recover the bodies from the Philistines; and then they gave to them as honourable a burial as was in their power. It might have been fairly anticipated that, on his coming into power, David would make an early effort to bring the body of Jonathan to his native place, and there inter it with all the honour befitting the burial of such a princely man and faithful friend. Instead of this, David allowed thirty years to pass away before he did what reverence and gratitude for the dead should have constrained him to regard as a sacred duty to be discharged as soon as possible. After that long period, he was awakened to a sense of what was becoming, by hearing of a widow's faithful service to the dead bodies of her children. This incident is eminently worthy of careful consideration, for it belongs to one of the strangest passages in David's chequered history, and it furnishes a very striking instance of the irresistible power of example.

Towards the close of David's life, the prosperity of the kingdom was interrupted by a famine. It seems that at first the king supposed it to arise from ordinary causes, and it awakened in him no special spiritual anxiety; but when it continued and increased in severity for three years, he accounted it to be a judgment from God, and sought to know for what reason it was inflicted. "*He inquired of the Lord. And the Lord answered, It is for Saul, and for his bloody house, because he slew the Gibeonites.*" It will be remembered that, in the days of Joshua, the Gibeonites had, by means of false pretences, obtained a covenant of peace between themselves and the Israelites. They were degraded to perpetual servitude; but with all the sacredness of a solemn oath the public faith was pledged to them for the security of their lives. Under circumstances not fully disclosed to us, Saul broke the oath and forfeited the honour of the nation, by slaying many of the Gibeonites, and by attempting to destroy them all.

It has been supposed by some that he was severe and cruel towards the Gibeonites, as a kind of set-off against his pretended compassion towards the Amalekites. A guilty severity on the one hand, to atone for a forbidden lenity on the other hand! It seems as silly as it was sinful; but then all sin is foolish as well as guilty; and a corrupt heart has power to muddle the best brain and to turn even a Solomon into a fool! Others have conjectured that Saul slew the Gibeonites at the same time that he slew the priests whose servants they were. Later commentators* have thought that light is to be obtained from the question Saul put to his courtiers when he was disclosing his suspicions against David: "*Hear now, ye Benjamites; will the son of Jesse give every one of you fields, and vineyards, and make you captains of thousands and captains of hundreds?*" This implies that Saul either had given or would give them fields and vineyards. It has been asked, "Where did Saul get land to distribute amongst his servants, as a means of securing fidelity to himself?" He could not have acquired it in his own country by purchase, or in neighbouring countries by conquest, but he could, and probably did, acquire it by dispossessing and destroying the Gibeonites. One thing is certain—the guilty deed was done in the alleged interest of the Jewish people; for it is said, "*Saul sought to slay them in his zeal to the children of Israel and Judah.*" It is easy to understand that the thing was popular with many of

* See Kitto's " Daily Bible Illustrations."

the Jews, for, if it did not enrich them, it humoured their prejudices, and gratified their not unnatural feelings of hostility toward the Gibeonites. Nothing is more likely than that the King perpetrated the flagrant crime in order to regain some of his lost popularity. It has too frequently happened that monarchs, who have not tried to win the affection and fidelity of their subjects by a wise and righteous use of power, have sought to gratify them by pandering to some evil passion. Herod killed James, the brother of John, with the sword; "*and, because he saw it pleased the Jews, he proceeded further to take Peter also.*" There are many reasons why we should pray for kings and for all that are in authority, and this is not the least of them—the more they use their power in wisdom and righteousness, the more they are shielded against temptations to abuse their power. Those who enthrone themselves in the hearts of the people by the equity and benignity of their sway, never have need to resort to the degrading and guilty expedient of making wars against other nations, and of wronging or plundering or abusing other people in order to be popular with their own subjects. With what awful force one sin drives a man on to another sin! If Saul had maintained his godliness, and done his duty, he would never have been tempted to murder his peaceful and unoffending vassals in order to show "his zeal to the children of Israel and Judah."

The sin of Saul was regarded by God as a national sin, either because the people shared in the plunder, or because they sympathised with or connived at the deed. The matter was one of double guilt, for, besides the shedding of innocent blood, there was the violation of a solemn compact. The breaking of oaths and promises is exceedingly sinful in the sight of Him who is infinitely faithful, and who, in His grace to the guilty, makes an everlasting covenant with them. It is quite possible that the treaty the

Jews had made was sometimes irksome to them; but faithfulness is not to limit itself to promises which are easy and pleasant to fulfil. "*Lord, who shall abide in Thy tabernacle? Who shall dwell in Thy holy hill? He that sweareth to his own hurt, and changeth not!*" The sin of the King and his people was not instantly followed by punishment, but the Lord patiently waited for confession and repentance. Year after year passed away, and the crime was neither mourned over nor acknowledged. It seemed to be forgotten by almost every one excepting Him into whose unforgeting memory every transgression enters, and who sets all our sins before Him, our secret sins in the light of His countenance. Nearly fifty years had expired, and still there was no sense of guilt—no reparation for wrong-doing. Then the Lord came forth to punish. He stayed the rains of heaven, the fields were parched, the harvest was scanty, and there began to be unsatisfied hunger and thirst in the land, which usually flowed with milk and honey. For three years these strokes of judgment were repeated with a constantly increasing severity, and in the school of experience the sinful people were taught the difference between the delay in punishment which Divine patience makes, and the forgiveness of sin which human penitence secures. "*These things hast thou done, and I kept silence: thou thoughtest I was altogether such an one as thyself. But I will reprove thee and set them in order before thine eyes.*" Some men have a feeling that there is an appearance of injustice if a crime be punished many years after its perpetration. But lapse of time has no power to diminish the guilt of an action, and why should it deter or diminish punishment? If lapse of time work change in the offender, bringing him to repentance, then it is meet for mercy to interpose with pardon, and keep back punishment for ever. This is according to God's promise: "*If the wicked restore the pledge, give again that he had robbed, walk in the statutes of life without committing iniquity; he shall surely live, he shall not die.*

None of his sins that he hath committed shall be mentioned unto him." Where, on the other hand, the rolling years reveal no improvement, the guilt is increased instead of diminished. To the guilt of the transgression in former days is now to be added the guilt of abusing the patience of God and frustrating the gracious purpose of His forbearance. In these cases delayed judgment will be at last heavier judgment. Lapse of time may lead us to forget a sin, or lose our sense of its sinfulness; but what is the lapse of a life-time in the sight of God? There is no pleading a statute of limitations in His courts. "*With Him a thousand years are but as yesterday when it is past, and as a watch in the night.*"

Of course objectors will ask the old question: "Was it just to make one generation suffer for the sins of another?" Seeing the famine did not come till more than forty years after the offence, the greater part of the offenders must have entirely escaped the punishment; and it is said, therefore, the delayed judgment must have been an unjust judgment. How is it people never think of asking this other question: "Is it just for one generation to be enriched in many ways by the skill and labour and victories of a preceding generation?" The law of God that links the generations together is constantly and powerfully working for good. We are all of us more or less better in body, mind, and estate, because of the virtues of those who have lived before us. If we were to be stripped of all the fruit of the various excellences of bygone generations, how poor and feeble we should be! How is it that the child of English Christian parents starts on the journey of life with a nature in many respects very distinct from and superior to the nature of the child of barbarian and pagan parents? It is because, from its very birth, the English child is benefited and blessed through the character its ancestors have maintained for generations past. Our freedom, our art and science, our civilization, with all its power to mitigate the sorrows and increase the pleasures of life, are not the creation of our wisdom, they are not the product of our virtues. By far the larger portion of them we owe, under God, to the work and worth of those who now sleep in their graves. "Other men laboured, and we have entered into their labours." We are always reaping golden grain which grows from good seed our fathers scattered; and therefore we must not be ready to impeach the Divine justice because sometimes we are torn by thorns and briers, which they, in their seasons of folly and sin, did plant. Instead of sitting in ignorant, presumptuous judgment on God's justice, let us be more careful to maintain our own. Is there one who complains of suffering which comes upon him through the sins of others? Then, in common fairness, he ought to complain also because he enjoys so much through the virtues of others. If he look at the thorns and briers our ancestors planted, and exclaim, "God ought not to let me be torn by these, I did not commit the folly of planting them!" he should also look at the broad harvest-field of English freedom, civilization, and religion, and exclaim, "God ought not to let me gather one sheaf from this paradisaic plenty; I had nothing to do with ploughing the soil and scattering the seed. No shed blood of mine ever became part of the red rain that made the harvest grow so fast!" Concerning the law which connects our characters and circumstances with those of our fathers, we should ask: "What! shall we receive good at its hand, and shall we not receive evil?" It was ordained of God in a benignant spirit, and for a beneficent purpose; and it is man's folly that turns it into a power for inflicting evil, and a channel along which calamities flow from the past to the present, and from the present to the future. Instead of cavilling at a law which we could not repeal, if we would, and ought not to repeal, if we could, let us always remember that the law is in force, and be constrained so to carry ourselves that those who come after us shall never have to suffer for our sins.

It was doubtless by God's direction that David suffered the surviving Gibeonites to decide what should be done to expiate the sin. They demanded that seven of Saul's descendants should be publicly executed, and their demand was granted. Saul and his sons had been the leaders in the unprincipled slaughter, and his descendants were most likely the largest holders of the unrighteous spoil. It was fitting that, if any were to suffer death for the sin, it should be these princes, and not some of the common people who had followed in the footsteps of their King. They were brought forth and hanged in the sight of all the land; and, in a very forcible manner, princes and people, statesmen and priests, were taught that the national honour must be kept inviolate, that the feeble must not be oppressed, that the strong must not confound might with right, and that wickedness must not go unpunished, because it gets into the high places of the earth.

It was contrary to Jewish custom to leave the bodies upon the gibbets to waste away; but it was done in the case of these seven, either because the Gibeonites demanded it, or in order to make the warning more terrible. It gave rise to a most touching display of motherly affection and fidelity. Two of the seven were sons of Rizpah, who, though she had been one of Saul's wives, was still living. If she had possessed the power, we may be sure she would have tenderly taken the bodies of her loved ones from the disgraceful gibbets, and have buried them in peaceful graves, which she would have wet with her tears till death had laid her to sleep by their side. She could not bear the thought of their hanging there for the vultures to tear to pieces and devour, and she determined to keep watch over them and drive off the foul birds of prey. The blackening corpses dangling in the air must have been a horrid spectacle to her, and we could not have wondered if she had fled away from the heart-breaking sight. But her love, prompting her to do what she deemed her duty to the dead, was mighty and triumphant over all. She made her home upon the rock, and watched with a vigilance that never slept, and a devotion that never wearied. In a few words the inspired historian sets before us such a scene as a poet's fancy never conceived, and a painter's pencil never adequately portrayed. "*And Rizpah took sackcloth, and spread it for her upon the rock, from the beginning of harvest until water dropped upon them out of heaven, and suffered neither the birds of the air to rest on them by day, nor the beasts of the field by night.*" They were counted as accursed, and unworthy of the burial of dogs; but she would not cast them out of her heart. The more they were shunned by others, the more she clung to them; and the deeper their disgrace, the deeper her compassion. It is a great thing when God say sthat He pities like a father; it is a far greater thing when He affirms that His love is more unforgetting and imperishable than the love of a woman to her own offspring!

It was told David what Rizpah had done, and instantly his memory was awakened, and his conscience was quickened. He thought of the bones of Saul and Jonathan sleeping in the place of their somewhat hurried and unseemly burial. He saw the duty he ought to have discharged years before, and he at once girded himself to discharge it. He fetched the long-neglected remains from Jabesh-Gilead, and carried them to the country of Benjamin, and buried them in the sepulchre of Kish, the father of Saul. With them he buried also the bodies of the seven, and thus relieved the tender and faithful-hearted Rizpah from the burden of work and woe which her love for her own had laid upon her. The history closes with these significant words: *"And after that God was entreated for the land."* Long-forgotten sin had been brought to mind, and acknowledged, and expiated; homage had been paid to justice; the evil of unfaithfulness had been exposed; the honour of the nation had been purged from foul stains; it had been shown that neither kings nor princes can do wrong with impunity; maternal fondness and fidelity had been touchingly displayed; a long-forgotten duty had been attended to; a noble example had borne fruit; and "*after that God was entreated for the land.*" The generous heavens poured down their showers, the languishing life of field and vineyard revived, and the earth was clothed with beauty and teemed with fruitfulness again. There was one more glorious proof of the everlasting truth— RIGHTEOUSNESS EXALTETH A NATION.

The way in which Rizpah's conduct moved David to his duty affords a fine instance of what has been aptly called "unconscious influence." She had no design upon the conscience of the King, but her right doing told with great effect. If she had lectured him about his duty to the sleeping dust of his friend, he might have resented her efforts as an impertinence; but he could neither resent nor resist the silent appeal of her actions. Words are often feeble and in vain, but deeds are seldom fruitless. The most eloquent preachers may have to cry out complainingly—"Who hath believed our report?" The success of example is far more certain, for its fragrance has never been a sweetness wholly "wasted on the desert air." Susceptibility to its power is a universal possession. Birds that have become dumb and have forgotten their strains, have had their memories touched, and have been moved to melodious songs again, by being placed where they could hear the carols of other birds. Did any man ever yet, by the grace of God, set his life to holy music, without stirring up the instinct of sacred song in some other human breast? NO MAN LIVETH TO HIMSELF! NO MAN DIETH TO HIMSELF!

VIII.

THE TWO THINGS WHICH DAVID HAD NEVER SEEN.

Psalm xxxvii. 25.

"I have been young, and now am old; yet have I not seen the righteous forsaken, nor his seed begging bread."

THE TWO THINGS WHICH DAVID HAD NEVER SEEN.

THERE can be no doubt that many disadvantages and disabilities belong to the period of old age. For many reasons, the season of youth is to be greatly preferred. In elasticity of limb, in buoyancy of feeling, in the intensity with which pleasure can be enjoyed, in the faculty of getting great mirth out of very small materials, in the irrepressible energy with which both body and spirit overflow, the young man has a decided advantage over the old one. In the midst of his present infirmities, the old man remembers the time when he too was in the pride of youth and prime of life, and possessed all the glories of an unwasted and unwearied nature; and as he realises that they have passed away from him for ever, so far as earthly experience is concerned, he cannot help a measure of pensiveness stealing over his spirit. But he soon checks his sadness by reminding himself that the goodness of the Creator has left no period of life without its own peculiar pleasures, and hence even old age has its own special advantages and alleviations. He knows that while the course of time has separated him widely from the energy and enthusiasm of youth, it has also enlarged his experience and matured his wisdom. He knows his own heart better than he formerly knew it, and is less likely to commit the folly of an excessive confidence in it. He knows the real nature and worth of things better, and is less likely to be deceived by mere appearances. He knows God better; and, therefore, with increased force, he can testify how safe it is to trust in God, how wise it is to serve Him, and what ever-multiplying reasons there are for loving Him with all the heart, and soul, and strength. In the most effective of all schools the old man has learned lessons of priceless value, which, apart from the teaching of years and circumstances, he could not have learned. He has the wisdom which is the offspring of experience, the best wisdom in the world for giving birth to patience and contentment, forbearance and charity. He waits for further light where a young man would rush to hasty conclusions. He knows how to do nothing and to say nothing in circumstances which would tempt a young man to say and to do all manner of rash things, whereby present difficulties would be complicated, and work would be provided for future repentance. "Thanks be to God!" he can exclaim, "the great law of compensation which runs through the universe prevails in all its beneficent force in these regions of old age. The same irresistible tide which has swept me away from some privileges and powers, has carried me into possession of others. My eye has become dim, and my natural force is abated, but I have treasures which belong to no other period of life.

These 'the hand of palsy shall never touch, and the fire of fever shall never burn.' The outward man decays, but the inward man is renewed day by day."

To a generous heart, delighting in doing good, it would be a great grief if no further service could be rendered. The old man is not doomed to that sadness. For him the change is not from usefulness to uselessness, but from one kind of service to another. As in earlier life he rendered effective help by his ardour, and vigour, and passion for work, so now he can serve by means of his sober counsels, ripened wisdom, and mature character. This was fully exemplified in the history of David. We have seen him serving his generation in circumstances wherein the strength and enthusiasm of the young man were necessary; and we have now to listen to him as in this psalm he serves all generations by bearing that emphatic testimony in favour of godliness, which is never so effective as from the lips of an old man. This is not a psalm in which David confesses his own sins, or celebrates his own mercies, or tells the troubles of his own life. It is rich in counsel given by the aged saint to other people. He exhorts them to be patient, and not to fret because wicked people sometimes prosper, and not to think that God cares nothing about the good or the evil of human character, and that godly people have nothing but the shady and wintry side of earthly life. He entreats them to wait on the Lord, to be faithful and diligent in all well-doing, and to set their hearts on holiness, counting that to be the greatest treasure man can gain or God can give. He assures them that this course must sooner or later prove the only wise and safe course. It may, for a while, lead through darkness and difficulty, but it will finally conduct the persevering pilgrim to peace and joy, to glory and to God. David gives these exhortations and assurances on the strength of his own experience and observation. These were the truths he had learnt during his long and chequered career. "*A little that a righteous man hath is better than the riches of many wicked. The steps of a good man are ordered by the Lord, and He delighteth in his way. Though he fall, he shall not be utterly cast down: for the Lord upholdeth him with His hand.* I HAVE BEEN YOUNG, AND NOW AM OLD; YET HAVE I NOT SEEN THE RIGHTEOUS FORSAKEN, NOR HIS SEED BEGGING BREAD."

It must be borne in mind that these words are not a Divine promise, but a human testimony; not a declaration on God's part as to His unchanging and universal purpose, but a statement on the part of one man as to his life-long experience. This fact prompts the inquiry—Who and what was this man? Before examining the nature of the testimony, we must look at the character and capacity of the witness. He tells us of two things he had never seen; but had he travelled far and wide, or had he looked round upon only a narrow circle? He declares that he never saw a good man in spiritual loneliness, or a good man's children in utter temporal destitution; but in what scenes and circumstances had he spent his days?

If he always consorted with the prosperous and the wealthy, the things he saw not may have existed not very far from him, although his heart was never troubled by the sight of them. There are people so enshrined in ease and splendour, that they know little or nothing of the world of want and woe which lies just outside of their charmed and gilded circle. That world is none the less real, because easy-going and pampered folk live in what they would deem blissful ignorance of it. Was the psalmist a man after this fashion? Was he of the number who, because they always sleep in the lap of luxury themselves, dream not of poverty and pain endured by others? The answer is, that there never lived a man who, by a wide and diversified experience, was better able than David to speak with authority upon the matter about which he here testifies. Supposing ourselves in his presence, we may inquire of him as to his fitness for bearing this testimony. From the facts of his wondrous history we can imagine what his answer would be.

"I am king of Israel, and I dwell in a palace of cedar. I have rest from all mine enemies round about me. There are thousands of men to whom my word is law, and of earthly good I have all that wealth can purchase, or power procure, or heart can wisely desire. But I have known other times, and lived in other circumstances. To what extreme of human position am I an utter stranger? To what height of power and prosperity have I not been uplifted? To what depth of sorrow and difficulty have I not been cast down? I was a peasant in Bethlehem; I married the king's daughter and became a prince of the realm. I have been keeper of a handful of sheep in the wilderness, and I have commanded the hosts of Israel in the field of battle. I have been the champion and deliverer of my fatherland, and I have been treated as its offscouring, to be cast out with scorn and violence. I have been the idol of the people, eulogised in their songs, greeted with their loud acclaim, enveloped in the clouds of their incense; I have been falsely denounced both as a traitor and a tyrant, and I have been hunted like a partridge upon the mountains. I have drunk the full cup of a conqueror's glory; I have tasted the bitterness of exile, and have barely escaped the martyr's death. I have lived in palaces; I have had to hide myself in dens and caves of the earth. I have had all things richly to enjoy, and I have known what it is to eat one's last piece of bread and not be able to tell whence the next meal will come. I have been blessed by Samuel, and cursed by Shimei. I have been the companion of crowned kings and inspired prophets; I have been captain of a band of discontented men, with whom debt and difficulty were the chief bond of union. I have been borne to the throne by the enthusiasm of a grateful people; I have been driven from it by a cruel rebellion, of which my own son was the leader. The faithfulness and loving-kindness of my God I have put to the test in all manner of scenes and circumstances. I have tried the worth of godliness always and everywhere. I have tried it in prosperity and in adversity,—in my father's

peaceful home, and amongst the uncircumcised Philistines,—in the time of my greatest popularity, and in the season of my fiercest persecution. I tried it in the noontide of my glory, when not one dark cloud spotted my azure sky, and not one forecast shadow of a coming trouble fell upon my path; I tried it in the midnight of my anguish, when my crown was stolen from me, and my favourite son was the thief,—when the sword was drawn against me, and my own son's was the hand that plucked it from the scabbard. I tried it on the top of my delectable mountains, where the consciousness of grace received, and duty discharged, and sin forsaken, and holiness acquired, gave me rich foretastes of the bliss of paradise; I tried it in the time of my remorse, when the prophet's parable awoke my slumbering conscience, when the arrows of conviction pierced my spirit, and when from my breaking heart there went up the cry which brought back pardon and peace,—
"*Hide Thy face from my sins, and blot out all mine iniquities: cast me not away from Thy presence, and*

take not Thy Holy Spirit from me.' Is there any extreme in human experience which is utterly unknown to me? Who has had a life richer than mine in strange and strong contrasts? Yet in all things and through all things and above all things, I have found that the Lord is mindful of His own. 'I HAVE BEEN YOUNG, AND NOW AM OLD; YET HAVE I NOT SEEN THE RIGHTEOUS FORSAKEN, NOR HIS SEED BEGGING BREAD.'"

"Take thy shoes from off thy feet, for the place whereon thou standest is holy ground!" It behoves us to bow ourselves before this aged man, and to receive his testimony with the utmost confidence. That which he passes on to us is no crude theory, no empty bubble blown by mere conjecture; it is solid gold which has been tried again and again in the crucible of life, and has come forth from the fire seven times purified. If David had said, "This is how I think it will be, and how I think it ought to be," we might have been tempted to reply, "Yes! but things are often appallingly different from our notions of what is likely and right." But when he says, "This is what I have observed during my long and eventful career," we must respond, "Thy words are weighty, thy testimony is trustworthy." Next to inspired declarations, we can have nothing more trusty than the lessons of human experience extending over a vast and varied range of events. History is man's best book of prophecy. That which has been, why should it not be repeated? Man's necessities and God's nature are the same. He who has hitherto cared for the righteous, and kept their children from destitution, is He not the Father of Lights, with whom is no variableness nor shadow of turning?

The fact of David's eminent fitness to bear witness on this matter reminds us of one great feature of the Bible. The message is always sent by the right messenger. In every case the words gather additional force and value from the circumstances or the character of the man by whom they were spoken. Words about the freeness and fulness of pardon would have been quite as true, but they would have been less weighty, if they had been spoken by those who showed no deep sense of the greatness of man's guilt. Isaiah and Micah make glorious declarations concerning the riches of Divine forgiveness, and their assurances are all the more encouraging to the penitent because both of them paint most appalling pictures of human depravity and defilement. The Apostle Paul says that earthly afflictions are light and momentary, and that heavenly bliss is an exceeding and eternal weight of glory. This estimate of the sorrows and troubles of the present life would have been scorned and repudiated by woe-stricken people if it had been put forth by a man who personally knew little of affliction. What force there is in the Apostle's words to those who remember that he who talked thus of burdens being light and lasting only for a moment, did himself endure enough to make a man a martyr ten times over! The human element in the Bible neither dims the brightness nor impairs the power of the Divine element. On the contrary, God in

His thoughtful love chose such channels for the transmission of the waters of life, that to us men they are all the more sweet and refreshing because of the particular human courses along which they flow.

From the capacity of the witness we now turn to see the meaning of his testimony. The first part of it is not difficult to understand or to receive: "I HAVE NOT SEEN THE RIGHTEOUS FORSAKEN." David could not say he had never seen a good man in straits and difficulties, for his own godliness had not kept him free from such things. He had seen the righteous heavily burdened, but he had never seen him left to carry his woe without sympathy or succour from his God. He could not say that he had never seen a good man in sorrow and darkness, for, in the days of its greatest vigour and purity, his own goodness had not secured him immunity from grief and gloom. Death had come into his house, and he had laid his loved ones in the grave. He had been almost wrecked on trouble's stormy sea, and had cried out to God,

"All Thy waves and Thy billows have gone over me." But he affirmed that in his greatest extremities a good man can say, "*The Lord of hosts is with me, the God of Jacob is my refuge. Yea, though I walk through the valley of the shadow of death, I will fear no evil; for Thou art with me, Thy rod and Thy staff they comfort me.*" David had seen the good man forsaken by his fellow-men, but even then he could say, "I am not alone." He had seen the righteous when his own flesh and blood turned against him, and when, through the power of popular clamour, even parental love had been somewhat impaired. He had never seen the good man when he could not say, "*Though father and mother forsake me, the Lord will take me up.*" He could not say he had never seen the righteous fall away from his steadfastness and wander from duty, for he himself had broken through the fences of the law and had madly gone astray. But even in such unworthiness and disgrace he had not been forsaken. In his very wanderings the goodness and mercy of the Lord followed him and brought him back, and put into his lips the song which fallen angel has never been able to sing, "*He restoreth my soul, He leadeth me in the paths of righteousness for His name's sake.*"

Within the limits of this lower creation, is not a good man the noblest work of God? Does not God, speaking of Himself after the manner of men, affirm that He has all a workman's fondness for His own handiwork, and all a parent's love for His own offspring? "*But now thus saith the Lord that created thee, and He that formed thee, Fear not; thou art mine. When thou passest through the waters I will be with thee. I have made, and I will bear, even I will carry and will deliver you.*" For the production and preservation of the righteous, what cost and care have been expended! Wherever we see true human goodness, we may fearlessly assert that for its creation and development, God has spoken by His prophets, He has ruled in His providence, He has wrought by His Spirit, and He has suffered in the person of His Incarnate Son. This should suffice to assure us that the righteous shall never be forsaken by their Creator and Redeemer. True love is not exhausted by labour. The love which has done but little for the loved ones may dwindle and die, but diligent and self-denying love is nourished by its own toils and sufferings. Yea, instead of being the destroyer of love, hard work is often the creator of love. When the motherless babe is left alone in the world, you do not, as you put it into the arms of a woman who is a stranger, bid her love it as if it were her own. You know it is useless to command affection; and therefore all you do is to make the stranger promise that she will work for the little one and watch over it. That is enough! If you can secure the work, you may be certain that the affection will follow. The daily labours and the nightly watchings for which you pay will sooner or later create the fondness you could not purchase in any market in the world; and the one and only woman on whom you may rely to love the child as its own mother would have loved it, is the woman who has tended it and toiled for it, who has had to bear with all its fretfulness and waywardness, and to be perpetually on the alert to guard it against danger and to satisfy its wants. It is a glorious fact in the history of the human heart, that in thousands of instances a mother-like love has sprung out of mother-like work. Was not the heart in which this is possible created in the image of God? Whenever we see human loving-kindness strengthened instead of exhausted by its own efforts and sacrifices, do we not behold a faint trace of the Divine image, a dim revelation of the glory of God's grace? We can say that Christ wrought and suffered for us because He loved us; may we not add that, if it were possible for His love to be increased, He would love us all the more because of what He has done and endured for us? If human love is too strong for work to wear it out, we may be assured that Divine grace cannot be destroyed or enfeebled by its own labours. St. Paul did not say:—"He that has given us so much, how can we expect Him to give us any more? He that has done so much for us, how can we think He will do anything more?" The Apostle's argument was the reverse of this, for he felt that faith is reason when, on the ground of what has already been done, the thought of desertion is rejected, and the continuance of God's presence and blessing is confidently expected. "*He that spared not His own Son, but delivered Him up for us all, how shall He not with Him also freely give us all things?*"

There is great force in the prayer which it is said was frequently used by Queen Elizabeth, "O Lord, look at the wounds in Thy hands, and then Thou wilt not forsake the work of Thy hands." The same plea is urged in the "Dies Iræ:"

> "Jesus, Lord, my plea let this be,
> Mine the woe that brought from bliss Thee;
> On that day, Lord, wilt Thou miss me?
>
> "Wearily for me Thou soughtest,
> On the cross my soul Thou boughtest;
> Lose not all for which Thou wroughtest."

Can there be more than one answer to that

appeal? Is it not predicted that His love and labour are not to be wasted, but that He is to see of the travail of His soul and be satisfied? "*The Lord will perfect that which concerneth me; Thy mercy, O Lord, endureth for ever; forsake not the works of Thine own hands.*" HE HATH SAID, I WILL NEVER LEAVE THEE NOR FORSAKE THEE. It is not strange then that, though David had such a varied experience and such a wide field of observation, he could say, "I HAVE BEEN YOUNG AND NOW AM OLD, YET HAVE I NOT SEEN THE RIGHTEOUS FORSAKEN."

IX.

THE TWO THINGS WHICH DAVID HAD NEVER SEEN.

(CONTINUED.)

PSALM xxxvii. 25.

"I have been young, and now am old; yet have I not seen the righteous forsaken, nor his seed begging bread."

THE TWO THINGS WHICH DAVID HAD NEVER SEEN.

(CONTINUED.)

THE piety which Divine power creates, Divine goodness doth richly recompense. It is ignorantly supposed by some that to speak of the rewards of human conduct is to imply the existence of human merit. They forget that what man's godliness may deserve is one thing, and what God in His love will give to it is another and a very different thing. It is true that the possession of holiness increases the *obligations* rather than the *claims* of men, for in every case it is the work and gift of God; yet, in the abundance of His mercy, He rewards it as fully as if it were highly meritorious on man's part. Hence

HAD ates, Divine nse. It is peak of the ly the exist- that what thing, and it is another rue that the he *obligations* n every case in the abun- as fully as if part. Hence while as a matter of human merit our godliness may be entitled to nothing, as a matter of Divine mercy it is entitled to "all things," and is encouraged by the "promise of the life that now is, and of that which is to come." One chief object of this psalm is to set forth some of the blessings secured to the good man, and thereby to show the superiority of his position, even in this world, over that of his ungodly neighbour. Amongst the manifold advantages of godliness, David gives prominence to this: it promotes the temporal prosperity of the children of its possessor. To such an extent does it do this, that in all his long life and chequered experience David had never seen the seed of the righteous begging bread. He had seen them in straits and difficulties, but never in deep and continued destitution. For their fathers' sake they have been so favoured by God and by men as to be kept from utter and abject want. While David speaks of his own observation only, he would evidently have us to understand that what he had noticed was not exceptional, but in harmony with the general course of things. Always and everywhere it may be expected that a good man's spiritual excellence will bring temporal blessings to his children, and some of the rich rewards of his piety will fall into the lap of his posterity.

In support of this position, explicit declarations of Scripture and Divine promises can be quoted. How frequently Abraham was encouraged by the assurance that the blessings wherewith his faith and obedience were to be crowned should descend to his posterity! In behalf of consistent piety the appeal was made to his parental affection as often as it was made to his lawful self-love. The promise of good repeatedly ran thus: "To thee and to thy seed after thee." In the 102nd Psalm the eternity of God is set forth in contrast with the perishableness of the heavens and the earth, and from the fact of His unchangeableness this consolatory conclusion is drawn: "The children of Thy servants shall continue, and their seed shall be established before Thee." In other forms the same truth frequently appears. "What man is he that feareth the Lord? His soul shall dwell at ease, and his seed shall inherit the earth. Blessed is the man that feareth the Lord, that delighteth greatly in His commandments. His seed shall be mighty upon earth. The generation of the upright shall be blessed. He will bless them that fear the Lord, both small and great. The Lord shall increase you more and more, you and your children. The mercy of the Lord is from everlasting to everlasting upon them that fear Him, and His righteousness unto children's children; to such as keep His covenant, and to those that remember His commandments to do them." It could have been no surprise to David to find the children of the godly kept from those depths of poverty into which others were plunged. He was prepared for such preservation, and when he witnessed it, he could joyfully exclaim, "This is just like the mercy of the Lord. It answers to His word. He is faithful that hath promised." Had he not God's authority for declaring that a good man's piety shall tell with beneficial power upon the circumstances of his descendants to the second and third generations, and that some of the Divinely appointed rewards of it shall be reaped by those who arise to bear his name and bless his memory. long, long after he has passed out of this mortal toil and strife into the peace and rest of heaven?

The world is full of proof that a bad man's badness is a hindrance to, and a blight upon, the prosperity of his children. Tens of thousands can be found, housed in poverty, clad in rags, steeped in ignorance, destitute of all bright prospects for this life; and no one can question that the folly and vice of their parents have been the fount and origin of their want and wretchedness. Of the multitudes of children now living in our workhouses—the big, cold homes which law has built for those for whom love has made no provision—there are many who inherit the pauper's hard lot because of calamities which could not be foreseen or averted: but a far larger number are there simply and solely through the sins of those who, having brought them into being, ought to have been as ministering angels spreading sheltering wings around them. In the filthy purlieus of all our great cities there are hosts of little ones of whom, despite all human neglect, it is, thanks be to God, still true that their angels always behold the face of their Father in heaven. But the dawning day awakes them to hunger and filth and terrible temptation; and when night wears towards its noon, they crawl into resting-places scarcely fit for a wild beast to lie down in. How does all this come to pass in a land of Christian light and almost fabulous wealth? In the great majority of cases there is but one explanation:—"*The fathers ate sour grapes, and the children's teeth are set on edge.*"

The constancy and the rigorousness with which this law operates in relation to evil, should assure us that it works with equal regularity and power in relation to good. We find that, under the government of an infinitely wise and gracious God, it is impossible for a man to be a bad man without thereby darkening the prospects and hindering the prosperity of his children. Under this same rule, must it not be at least equally impossible for a man to be a godly man without thereby brightening the prospects and promoting the prosperity of his children? Who can believe that the God who is Love has ordained and keeps in action a law which is more constant and mighty in cursing wickedness than in blessing righteousness? It is plain enough that He has made the relation between parent and child a free and open channel for the transmission of some of the sad consequences of evil doing. It would be blasphemy to believe that the channel is not as broad and unobstructed when some of the rewards of well-doing would flow from sire to son. Is not judgment His strange work, and mercy His delight? What is the first glimpse of God in relation to man which the inspired history gives us? We do not see Him planting a wilderness with thorns and briers for the punishment of man's disloyalty and transgression. He appears preparing and perfecting a paradise for the home of man's innocence and the reward of man's obedience. In all its subsequent revelations the Word shows that His joy is not to threaten, but to promise; not to destroy, but to save. The tears that Jesus wept over the coming doom of Jerusalem, were they not the tears of "God manifest in the flesh," a revelation of the Divine heart, and of the deep grief which is there when woe and curse have to be inflicted? The more we know of God, the more confidently we must come to the conclusion, that every new fact which shows He is still fulfilling His reluctant threatening, and "*visiting the iniquities of the fathers upon the children,*" is a fresh proof that the corresponding promise can never fail. Whether we can discern it or not, it must be true, that to those who fear Him the mercy of the Lord is everlasting, and HIS RIGHTEOUSNESS IS UNTO THEIR CHILDREN'S CHILDREN.

The history of David's posterity furnishes some striking facts in proof of his declaration. He served his generation according to the will of God, and then fell asleep. Long after he slept with his fathers, it went well with his children for his sake. Both his son and his grandson found the Divine remembrance of his piety coming as a shield between them and the strokes of punishment their sins had provoked. Solomon's consistency perished in the midst of his great prosperity.

> "He stood the storms when waves were rough,
> But in a sunny hour fell off,
> Like ships that have gone down at sea,
> When heaven was all tranquility."

He broke his vows, polluted the holy city with heathen abominations, and again corrupted the people whose purification had required so much of fiery trial. He richly deserved to lose the regal power which he had learnt to abuse so fearfully; but when, on account of his own sins, he ought to have been stripped of his splendour, he was suffered to wear it still because of the saintliness of his departed father. The Lord said, "*I will not take the whole of his kingdom out of his hand, but I will make him a prince all the days of his life,* FOR DAVID MY SERVANT'S SAKE, BECAUSE HE KEPT MY COMMANDMENTS AND MY STATUTES." Rehoboam came to the throne, and speedily made it clear that he was the son, not of the first and wise, but of the second and foolish Solomon. He was a sorry specimen of parental training, and serves to show that Solomon could write much better than he acted in relation to the bringing up of children. In one period of his life Solomon gave most godly counsel, and at another period he set a most ungodly example. It was then as it has been ever since, the good advice was no match for the bad example, and with the latter the power and the victory went. There would have been little room for wonder, and less for complaint, if Rehoboam had lost his kingship altogether. He would have lost it wholly if God had not dealt graciously with him out of regard to his godly ancestor. The promise was fulfilled, "*He shall have one tribe* FOR MY SERVANT DAVID'S SAKE."

The instincts and practices of men support the assertion that a good man's children will be succoured for his sake. The family of Saul passed through strange vicissitudes. In the time of difficulty and distress they were helped because of Jonathan's good name and fragrant memory. When amidst the successes and popularity of the new royal house, the members of the discrowned family were so likely to be forgotten, they were preserved from that bitterness, for David said, "*Is there yet any that is left of the house of Saul, that I may show him kindness for Jonathan's sake?*" The poor crippled son of the dead saint was brought out of his obscurity and poverty and made to dwell like a prince in the palace, and for many years the "kindness of God" was shown unto him by David. This is not cited as a proof of eminent saintliness or extraordinary generosity on the part of David. It was only an act of simple humanity, and hearts not specially touched by the grace of God would most likely have been prompted to a similar course. There are many who are now receiving the bounty of this nation, awarded to them not for their own sakes, but for the good character or services of their kindred. Sons and daughters of men of art, or science, or literature, are placed on the pension list as a tribute to the memory and as an acknowledgment of the labours of their fathers. There are circumstances under which the most rigid republican and economist could scarcely object to the bestowment of hereditary honours and endowments. When our Indian Empire was all but plucked from our hands, there was one whose heroism, combined with holiness, touched the people into a perfect enthusiasm of gratitude; but it was soon found, to the sorrow of the nation, that he had passed beyond the reach of its praises, and had been called by God to receive such a crown as earth can never give. Who thought of objecting when some of the rewards were bestowed on his son? It was felt by all to be a right thing to honour the piety and patriotism of the good man in the circumstances of his children. To how many young men the sympathy, and confidence, and kindness secured for them by their father's piety have been a large part of their capital, by the wise investment of which they have made ample fortunes. How often, when the prodigal's own conduct has power only to excite indignation and shut men's hearts against him, they cannot refuse all help to him because the image of his sainted father comes before their minds! We might not be able to justify this in every case by a series of elaborate arguments; but, in relation to many things, we deem our instincts to be as safe a guide as our reason; and our best instincts are strongly in favour of helping the seed of the righteous for the sake of the righteous.

The experience of multitudes who are enjoying prosperity may be cited in support of the Psalmist's declaration. If they had not been favoured with godly parents, they would not have had that preparation for the race, and that fair start, which have helped them to reach the goal. How many there are to whom, in one respect, it is an easy thing to obey the Master's bidding about taking no anxious thought for the morrow! Their morrow is, as to worldly good, so well provided for, they have no temptation to be over-careful about it. They owe this largely to the godliness of those who went before them. True religion came into the homes and hearts of their ancestors, and became the foremost labourer in laying the foundations and raising the superstructure of that palatial prosperity in which they now dwell. What thousands there are who, as they rest in the peace, and revel in the brightness, and rejoice in the plenty, wherewith their homes are filled, must exclaim, if they will tell all the truth, "It would not have been thus with us if there had not been fathers to pray for us, and to bequeath to us the inheritance of their good name!" You think of the companions of your childhood who are your companions no longer. Differences in circumstances, and still greater differences in character, have made a gulf between them and you, across which you and they never grasp hands and greet one another for the sake of "auld lang syne." You went to the same school with them; you played in the same streets; you rambled with them through field and woodland; and were wild with the same joy when spring-tide came to clothe the earth with beauty and flood the air with song. What then has wrought to make your present destiny so unlike to theirs? One great cause of the difference is found in the fact that when nightfall came you went to a home very unlike to theirs. They had no holy atmosphere surrounding their childhood. They had no godly mother to take them to her knees and tell them of Him who blessed the little ones. They had no godly father whose character lifted them into a better position, and opened up for them pathways to prosperity. These mercies, denied to them, were granted to you; and that is one chief reason why the stream of your life has had such a different course from theirs, and has of late years flowed through the midst of a fertile and felicitous region whose remotest borders the streams of their lives have never once skirted! The blessing that comes from a godly ancestry has been with you all your days, and your history is one long proof that *a good man leaves an inheritance to his children's children.*

This truth should remind us of the debt we owe to godliness. It has unquestionably brought to us many of the blessings of this life. It has placed us on vantage ground, multiplied our opportunities, and facilitated our successes. It has claims upon our service and our self-denial which ought to be irresistible. We should deem no sacrifice too great to be made in its interests. Few things are to be more reprobated than the conduct of those prosperous people who faithlessly forsake and flippantly sneer at the religion to which, in the lives of their ancestors, they owe their wealth and position. By many young men, proud of the money which other people gained for them, it is thought to be a great mark of superiority to disdain the community and the church wherein their fathers secured and sustained the godliness which had so much to do with their secular success. If, before they thus scorn religion, these young men would strip themselves of all that which, by God's blessing, they owe to it, they would have little wealth left for the nourishment of their pride; and some of them would soon have to inquire for the residence of the relieving officer of their parish.

The truth David brings before us should guide us in the action of our parental affection. We often ponder and plan and toil for the welfare of our little ones, when, if we were alone in the world, we should forego labour and take our ease. There is one way wherein we can, without fail, promote their prosperity: it is by the careful culture of our own piety. Lawful self-love and parental love need not impel us in different directions. We need not wish ourselves accursed for our children's sakes. The nearer to God we rise, the more like Christ we live, the holier men and women we become, the more certainly we shall secure blessings for those who will bear our names and stand in our places when our bodies sleep in the dust. It is as strange as it is true, that many parents are tempted to do inconsistent and un-Christian things with the hope of thereby promoting the temporal welfare of their children. Numbers who have made shipwreck of conscience would never have done dishonourable and dishonest things for the sake of bettering their *own* circumstances. It was for their children they did them. Their sons had social aspirations, and their daughters had costly tastes, which they were anxious should be realised and gratified; and in their fondness they went astray, and lost their own characters in their endeavours to benefit their children. Whoever does an ungodly thing, or a questionable thing, from such a motive, violates true expediency as well as sound principle. The blunder is almost as big as the sin, when the saintly consistency of the parent is sacrificed on the altar of the child's secular prosperity. In Sir Thomas More's days there were judges who sold justice; but in his greater wisdom he said to his family, "For your sakes

I must be an honest man, that I may leave you the rich inheritance of a father's good name."

Children, as well as parents, may learn their duty from this truth. Too frequently by their foolish ambition, and by hankering after greater show and luxury, they become tempters to their fathers. They help to widen the expenditure till it becomes increasingly difficult to provide things honestly. They create the supposed necessities to meet which parents make haste to be rich, and fall into many a hurtful snare. Amongst the shattered reputations over which one has had to mourn, not a few have been those of professedly Christian fathers, to whom the extravagant habits and tastes of their children became a hundred-handed devil, pushing them further and further away from rectitude into ruin. For their own welfare's sake, children should do all they can to encourage their parents in the culture of all Christian nobleness and the maintenance of all godly consistency. When the parent fails in righteousness, the children must suffer loss. It shuts them out from all share of the hope and joy inspired by this teaching of experience:—"I HAVE BEEN YOUNG, AND NOW AM OLD; YET HAVE I NEVER SEEN THE RIGHTEOUS FORSAKEN, NOR HIS SEED BEGGING BREAD."

X.

THE "LAST WORDS" OF DAVID.

2 SAMUEL xxiii. 1—5.

"Now these be the last words of David. David the son of Jesse said, and the man who was raised up on high, the anointed of the God of Jacob, and the sweet psalmist of Israel, said, The Spirit of the Lord spake by me, and His word was in my tongue. The God of Israel said, the Rock of Israel spake to me, He that ruleth over men must be just, ruling in the fear of God. And he shall be as the light of the morning, when the sun riseth, even a morning without clouds; as the tender grass springing out of the earth by clear shining after rain. Although my house be not so with God; yet He hath made with me an everlasting covenant, ordered in all things, and sure: for this is all my salvation, and all my desire, although He make it not to grow."

THE "LAST WORDS" OF DAVID.

ACCORDING to a commonly received interpretation of this passage, David mourned over the ungodly state of his children, but exulted in the assurance of his own personal salvation. He first repeated the description he had received from the Lord of the character which kings and rulers should maintain, and it is supposed that he next lamented the fact that his children did not answer to the Divine ideal. It is further supposed that his sorrow on account of their shortcomings instantly gave place to grateful joy in the hope that, through the mercy and faithfulness of God, he himself should be secure and blessed for ever. It might go ill with his children, but it would be well with him. They were godless, but he would none the less receive grace. "*Although my house be not so with God, yet He hath made with me an everlasting covenant, ordered in all things and sure.*" There are well-known facts in David's history which may seem to lend some sanction to this interpretation. His family troubles were great and many. Some of his children were anything but what his conscience could approve and his heart could desire. They were thorns in his side and arrows in his heart. Their wickedness must have embittered his cup for years, and have flung over his path a gloomy shadow which reached down to the grave. He had long and repeated experiences of the truth of the proverb: "*A foolish son is the calamity of his father.*" As he thought of Amnon and Absalom and Adonijah, he might well exclaim: "My house is not with God as it ought to be!" Still, is it not incredible that David, as he contemplated the lost condition of his children, could instantly get comfort by thinking of his own safety? He was sometimes sadly unlike his true self, but assuredly he was never so unlike himself as to say in effect, "My children may perish, but, the Lord be praised, I shall get to heaven myself!" This must be deemed impossible to David, even by those who take the worst view of his conduct in the matter of Uriah the Hittite. Those who know most of the generous and self-forgetting love which glows in the parental heart, will be the first to acquit David of that charge of intense selfishness which the common interpretation of the passage implies against him. They would be prepared to hear the exclamation: "My hope is robbed of much of its sweetness and power because my children are not embraced by it. How can I be happy in the prospect of a salvation from which those dearer to me than my own life are to be for ever excluded? How can heaven be to me a place of 'fulness of joy,' if all my loved ones are not with me there?" This is a mystery which only the light and experience of eternity can make clear. It has pressed with terrible power on the hearts of saintly parents. And who can doubt that it often troubled the spirit of David also? How much he loved his children,—yea, how he prized their safety, if possible, more than his own,—is made manifest by that outburst of grief: "*O my son Absalom, my son, my son Absalom! Would God I had died for thee, O Absalom, my son, my son!*"

There is another interpretation of the passage which makes it chiefly and almost exclusively a prophecy of Christ. It is supposed to regard Him as the King ordained of God, and to describe the perfection of His kingly character, the righteousness of His rule, the benignity of His sway over those who submit to it, and the destructive effects of His sovereignty upon those who are rebellious and disobedient. Those who adopt this interpretation make certain changes in the translation of the passage which remove from it everything like lamentation on David's part:—

> "Is not my house so with God?
> For He hath made with me an everlasting covenant,
> Ordered in all things and sure.
> For it is all my salvation and all my desire,
> Shall He not make it to flourish?"—FAIRBAIRN's *Typology*.

According to this translation David first describes the regal perfection and glory of the Saviour, and then rejoices in his own house (or dynasty) as being in its righteous character and beneficial influences an illustrious type of the Kingship of Jesus. In favour of this rendering great names may be quoted. It is free from the objections which are so fatal to the commonly received interpretation: and it will be especially grateful to those who love to get frequent glimpses of Jesus in the Psalms and Prophecies, and who, if they are to err at all, would far sooner go astray with those who find Him everywhere than with those who find Him nowhere in the Old Testament.

There is a third interpretation according to which David here sets forth the Divine ideal of a ruler over men as he in early life received it from the Spirit of the Lord. Now that he has reached the close of his kingly career, he compares that career with the description of a good king which God had given to him, and he finds that he has fallen far short of it. When he speaks of his "house" not being "so with God," he does not mean his domestic circle, but the reigning dynasty, and he refers, not to the godless character of his children, but to the imperfections of his own kingship. *That* had not been altogether such as God had enjoined, and as he himself had desired and determined. When he speaks of the "covenant ordered in all things," he exults, not in the thought that he is personally safe despite the irreligion of his children, but in the assurance that he shall be saved despite his shortcomings and failures as a king. The mercy of God would cover up all the imperfections and pardon all the sins of his government. While considering that the passage refers primarily and directly to David and his history as the Lord's anointed, we need not necessarily deny its Messianic character. Like every other picture of human perfection, this description of a perfect King was indirectly a prophecy of Christ, and the glorious ideal was fully realized, not in David, nor in Solomon, nor in Hezekiah, but only in David's greater Son.

These "last words" reveal to us the lofty standard of kingly character which was set before David in early life. In the rejection of Saul there was no arbitrary exercise of God's sovereignty. The son of Kish was weighed in the balances and found wanting. After his first great failure, the long-suffering of the Lord gave him further trial; but he soon failed again most grievously, and proved himself unfit for the throne. Like many other monarchs, he found it easier to remember that he was the king of the people than to remember that he was the servant of God. He was bent on having his own way, and he would wield his sceptre as if it were absolutely his own, and not a trust that he had received from the "King of kings and the Lord of lords." When he first flagrantly failed, Saul was threatened that a successor should be speedily found who would be a man after God's own heart; and when he failed yet more flagrantly, the threat was executed, and Samuel was sent to anoint one of the sons of Jesse. We may be certain that when David was set apart for the throne, he was not left in ignorance of the reasons of Saul's rejection. Samuel, who knew the sad story so well, and was so much grieved by it, would, with great pathos and power, relate it to David, and warn him against the rock of wilful disobedience on which Saul had suffered shipwreck. The venerable prophet, whose patriotic zeal for Israel's welfare flourished in such immortal vigour, would take pains to instruct David as to the duties and responsibilities of the kingly office, and would remind him that he might, by disloyalty to God, or by injustice to the people, forfeit the throne, even as Saul had lost it. After he was anointed, David went back to the sheepfolds, but, though he returned to his former occupation for a season, he could not be forgetful of his future destiny. He must have often thought of the greatness in store for him; and doubtless he often strove to realize what he should have to be and to do when that promised greatness came to him. We may lawfully suppose hat it was when he was in one of these meditative moods that light from heaven came into his mind, and he heard the Spirit of God speak to his spirit, and tell him what kind of a king he must be if he would answer to the noble title given to him when he was chosen—"A man after God's own heart." To some such revelation received in early life he must have referred, when, in old age, he exclaimed: "*The God of Israel said, the Rock of Israel spake to me, He that ruleth over men must be just, ruling in the fear of God.*"

Righteousness towards men and reverence towards God are named as the two great essentials in a good king. For lack of these, monarchs have been curses instead of blessings, and peoples have been oppressed, and kingdoms have been ruined. But where the authority of God has been recognized, and the rights of the people have been respected, nations have flourished, and kings have been a terror to evil-doers, and a praise to them that do well. Stress is laid upon justice rather than upon compassion, and history warrants the emphasis. If there were more righteousness in the world, there would be less need of charity. "The acts of charity are, to a great extent, counterworks to the operations of injustice. Let all the debts of justice be by all men discharged; let every man be just to himself and to all others; and then the spirit of mercy will have little to do but to look upon society with the smile of congratulation." It should never be forgotten that the favourite Scripture designation of a true saint is "a righteous man." The justice of the king is to be in association with the fear of God. This last named virtue is the only one that guarantees the perfection and permanence of all the rest. It is the only legitimate master-principle, and its presence and power secure that all other excellences shall be in proper order and in due proportion.

The benignant influence of a God-fearing and righteous ruler is described in expressive figurative language. Gladness and growth shall characterize his reign, for "*he shall be as the light of the morning, when the sun ariseth, even a morning without clouds;*

as the tender grass springing out of the earth by clear shining after the rain." Several years elapsed before the throne promised to David came into his possession; and it is probable that this vivid picture of kingly perfection was also placed before him some time prior to his accession. If so, how often he would gaze upon it while he was waiting for the kingdom, and what promises he would make of conformity to it! And when he was actually seated on the throne, how frequently he would recall the words of the Spirit, and assure himself that they should be the law of his life down to the last moment of the sceptre being in his hands!

These last words reveal to us the sad consciousness which David had in his old age, that the lofty standard set before him in early life had not been reached. His kingship was anything but a great failure. He conducted the affairs of the kingdom with much vigour and wisdom, and was instrumental in the fulfilment of many Divine promises, and in the advancement of many Divine purposes, relating to the chosen nation. He made six thousand of the Levites officers and judges, and systematically distributed them through the country for the education and elevation of the people and the better administration of justice."* It is said that there is a proverb amongst the Russians, which is quoted when in the remoter parts of the Empire justice is violated, oppression is practised, and crimes are committed: "God is high, and the Emperor is afar off." This proverb recognizes the truth that wrong and violence are likely to prevail in any district in proportion to its distance from the central seat of government. Against this danger David made provision by sending nearly half the six thousand Levites, the "chief fathers," as they were called, into that part of his kingdom which lay on the other side of Jordan.† In 1 Chron. xxvii. there is a list of officers appointed by David to superintend and improve the agriculture of the country, so that its material resources might be fully developed and economically used. He cul-

---

* 1 Chron. xxiii. 4. † 1 Chron. xxvi. 32.

tivated friendly relations between his own people and the Tyrians, in order to give the Jews a knowledge of the higher and more refined arts of civilised life. These facts show that while David was essentially a military monarch, he did not neglect home reforms for the sake of foreign wars; he subdued the enemies of Israel and took full possession of the land promised to their fathers, but, while he was extending the boundaries of his kingdom, he looked well to its internal arrangements. In promoting the civilisation and providing for the political welfare of the people, he did not forget that "righteousness exalteth a nation," and that `the rightness of men toward God is the great fountain of their rightness toward one another. He therefore paid attention to the ecclesiastical arrangements of his kingdom, and both by his psalms and his example he sought to advance pure and undefiled religion.

It cannot be questioned, then, that David's reign was a great blessing to the Jews, and that in the review of his career there was much to inspire him with joy and thankfulness. It was unspeakably superior to the reign of Saul, and would have compared most favourably with that of any one of his contemporaries. And yet the retrospect could not give him perfect satisfaction. He wisely abstained from comparing himself with his predecessor, or with the monarchs of surrounding nations. He did not give his conscience an unholy comfort by saying that he was as good as his neighbours. He looked at his kingly work in the light of his own early aims and promises. Alas! what a difference there was between his aspirations and his achievements! What a painful contrast between the hopes of youth and the memories of old age! He had to bow in penitential sorrow as he exclaimed, "The good that I would, I have not done." He tried his kingly work, not by the low standard current amongst pagan kings, but by the lofty standard the Judge of all the earth had set before him. Alas! what a difference between the Divine ideal and the human reality! When it was seen in the twilight of human notions his regal life might not only pass muster, but also call forth applause. When it was seen in the strong light of God's law—the light that shall fall on all human performances in the day of doom—what flaws, what stains, what defects, what deformities, were visible! Then he had to confess failure and to cry out, "My house is not so with God!" He had to deprecate judgment and appeal to mercy—"If Thou, Lord, shouldest mark iniquities, O Lord, who shall stand?" It was then that he exclaimed, "The limits of human goodness are very narrow, and the requirements of Thy law reach far, far beyond, into regions where the feet of man's obedience have never yet travelled! *I have seen an end of all perfection, but Thy commandment is exceeding broad.*"

Earthly perfection is one of the pleasant dreams of inexperience. It is generally the honest determination of young beginners to do very great things, and they firmly believe that all their lofty aspirations will be fully realised. This is one of the illusions of life by which every new generation is fascinated despite all the disappointments of preceding generations. Each fresh comer into the field is blissfully forgetful of human frailties and heroically defiant of difficulties, and nothing but his own personal experience will be able to shake his faith in the splendour of his future achievements. He will not relinquish his belief that perfection is to recompense his efforts until repeated failures hurl to the dust the gorgeous pile of his glowing expectations. What man ever yet accomplished all he purposed, either in relation to personal improvement or Christian usefulness? Even the apostle who, by Divine help, did more than most men to enrich the world, and lift himself nearer to God, had to confess, in old age, that the perfection to which he had aspired was still far away. He had not either in holy beauty or benignant influence made his life what, in bygone years, he meant and hoped to make it.

There never lived but One in this world whose review of His earthly life was free from all the sadness which sight of fault and failure brings.

When Jesus hung upon the cross, He could think of such a work as had never been devolved upon man or angel, and of that matchless work He could say, "It is finished!" He came into the world with the most perfect ideal of what He should be and of what He should do. He was all that He purposed to be! He did all He purposed to do! Glorious Gospel truth, that His perfection is not for our condemnation but for our justification! By the obedience of the One the many are to be made righteous. Glorious Gospel hope, that His disciples are to be conformed to His perfection in heaven! In the better land David and all His other servants shall have reviews of life furnishing materials for joy, and praise, and confidence, and hope. The grace of God, to which David turned for solace when the thought of life's failures made him sad, has pledged itself not only to forgive the earthly past, but also to make perfect the heavenly future. "As we have borne the image of the earthly, we shall also bear the image of the heavenly." What bliss there must be for those who have been for centuries in heaven, and whose memories, revisiting centuries of celestial life and labour, find in them obedience to every commandment, the fulfilment of every early promise, and the accomplishment of every high promise! To that perfect life which His love will give us beyond the grave, God's Word directs the hope of every one who is troubled in spirit and broken in heart by the memories of this faulty life, and who cries out in agony,—

> "When shall I, Lord, a journey take
> Through my departed years,
> And not a mournful visit make,
> And not return in tears?"

NEW WORKS

PUBLISHED BY

ELLIOT STOCK, 62, PATERNOSTER ROW, E.C.

Now ready, handsomely bound in cloth, price 5s., post free,

Baptist History,

FROM THE FOUNDATION OF THE CHRISTIAN CHURCH TO THE PRESENT TIME.

BY J. M. CRAMP, D.D.
Author of the "Text Book of Popery," &c.

WITH AN INTRODUCTION BY REV. J. ANGUS, D.D.

DR. CRAMP'S "Baptist History" is the only *complete* History of the Baptists issued in this country; its comprehensiveness, accuracy, and research render it the most reliable work on the subject, and its interesting details, popular style, and lucid arrangement, make it most attractive for popular reading. While interesting to general readers, it has special interest for members of Baptist churches and congregations; and it is hoped that these will interest themselves in the diffusion of the work in their own circles, especially among the young people in families and Sunday-schools, where far too little is known of the noble struggles and bitter persecutions which our forefathers sustained while upholding principles which they held dearer than life.

ELLIOT STOCK, 62, PATERNOSTER ROW, LONDON, E.C.

New Works Published by

Now ready, in crown 8vo., price 3s. 6d., post free,

Ancient Maxims for Modern Times.

By the Rev. HUGH STOWELL BROWN.

Contents.

I. Answering and Not Answering.
II. Have Your Revenge.
III. The Prosperity of Fools.
IV. Weights and Measures.
V. On Mocking and Being Mocked by Sin.
VI. The Keeping of the Heart.
VII. On Buying and Selling the Truth.
VIII. Family Quarrels.
IX. Honesty and Honour Towards God.

This excellent work is very beautifully printed in old face type, with ornamental antique headings, on toned paper, is handsomely bound in antique patterned mauve cloth, and will be found a most suitable and useful volume for presentation to young and old.

"A handsome volume of Divine maxims, illlustrated and enforced by one whose competency for the duty no one will dispute." —*Baptist Messenger*.

In fcap. 8vo, extra cloth, bevelled, price 3s. 6d., post free,

Living unto God :

CHAPTERS ON THE CHRISTIAN LIFE.

By the Revs. Dr. Steane, B. P. Pratten, W. J. Rosevear, S. Cox, J. H. Hinton, Chas. Vince, W. Landels, F. Tucker, J. Culross, J. Aldis, jun., S. G. Green, N. Haycroft, J. W. Lance, A. McLaren, E. White, O. Winslow.

"This volume, consisting of selections from the works of many writers, is eminently adapted to be useful. Eighteen of the best preachers of the day are severally made to contribute to the object and to the public good. It may be likened to an assemblage of ministers for spiritual converse, every one having his topic assigned him, and every one having spoken on that topic to the best of his ability."—*British Standard*.

ELLIOT STOCK, 62, PATERNOSTER ROW, LONDON, E.C.

Elliot Stock, 62, Paternoster Row.

A STORY OF GREAT INTEREST FOR BAPTISTS.

Now ready, price 3s. 6d., post free,

Theodosia Ernest;
OR, THE HEROINE OF FAITH.

A Story. Illustrated with numerous Full-page Engravings.

Many who would not read an abstract treatise on the subject of Baptism have, by reading this story, been led to feel an interest in it; and, while they have been entertained by the interesting circumstances of the tale, have been led to embrace the principles it is written to inculcate.

It is hoped that those who feel an interest in the spread of Scriptural truth in regard to Baptism, and especially those who wish to bring the subject before the young in a popular and attractive form, will take an interest in the circulation of the tale as it is now issued.

"A book not unlikely to bring over to our views and practices some who are not yet with us. It is certain to become a general favourite in the families where it is introduced, and we hope that it will be selected by the managers of our Sunday-schools, as one of the presents made to the elder scholars."—*General Baptist Magazine.*

Crown 8vo., cloth extra, price 5s., post free,

Calls to the Cross.

Being a Volume of Sermons preached at Manchester.

By the Rev. ARTHUR MURSELL.

"The present volume contains nineteen discourses of consummate ability, eminently fitted to do good both to the Church and to the world, raising and invigorating the piety of the one, and arresting the folly and working conviction in the souls of the other."—*British Standard.*

ELLIOT STOCK, 62, PATERNOSTER ROW, LONDON, E.C.

New Works Published by

THE NEW SUNDAY-SCHOOL CYCLOPÆDIA.

Now ready, price 4s. 6d., handsomely bound in cloth, post free,

The Sunday-School World,

An Encyclopædia of Facts and Principles, Illustrated by Anecdotes, Incidents, and Quotations from the Works of the most Eminent Writers on Sunday-School Matters.

Edited by JAMES COMPER GRAY,
Author of " Topics for Teachers," &c.

This work is designed to be a reference book for all who are engaged in the work of Sunday-school instruction; containing, in a condensed and classified form, practical information and counsel on *all* matters concerning the Sunday-school and its work. It will form a standard guide for Superintendents and Teachers, Secretaries, Librarians, Visitors, Treasurers, &c., &c., to the efficient conduct of every department and detail of their work.

The work is divided into the following sections:—1. The Institution itself. 2. The Superintendent and the Secretary. 3. The Teacher. 4. Matters relating to the Scholar. 5. The Infant Class. 6. Children's Services. 7. The Library and the Librarian. 8. Auxiliary Agencies. 9. Encouragements.

"It is very full of information, the selections made being not for length or the mere name of the author, but because of the facts and thoughts they supply. There does not exist any other work of the kind, and we gladly recommend it."—*Halifax Courier.*

*** Superintendents taking twelve copies are presented with one copy free.

Now ready, 176 pages, price 1s., post free,

Sermons for all Classes.
By REV. T. M. MORRIS.

" Full of earnest thought; the style is forcible and manly, and they are entitled with truth 'Sermons for all Classes.' "—*Pulpit Analyst.*

ELLIOT STOCK, 62, PATERNOSTER ROW, LONDON, E.C.

Elliot Stock, 62, *Paternoster Row.*

Now ready, post 8vo, cloth, price 6s.,

The Christian Policy of Life.

By REV. J. BALDWIN BROWN,
Author of "The Home Life," &c., &c.

CONTENTS:—1. The Fundamental Maxim. 2. Self-Discipline. 3. Self-Culture. 4. The Inner Circle—Home and Friends. 5. The Outer Circle—Business and the State. 6. On Getting on in Life. 7. The Lessons of the Birds and the Lilies. 8. On Release from Care. 9. Why should a Living Man Complain? 10. The Lights and Shadows of Experience. 11. On Living for Eternity.

"A sturdy book, and well calculated to help youth, to whom Mr. Brown dedicates it, to make men of themselves. We know of no writer who can better make language to bristle with thought. He writes so earnestly that his very soul seems to leap up through his words. He speaks as if from the depths of his own religious consciousness directly to you."—*Literary World.*

A VALUABLE BOOK FOR ALL BIBLE READERS.

Now ready, in Two Volumes, price 3s. 6d. each, post free, printed on toned paper, and handsomely bound in the best cloth, gilt, with 200 Illustrations, and eight well-executed Maps,

Topics for Teachers.

A BIBLE DICTIONARY,	A BIBLE COMMENTARY,
A BIBLE MANUAL,	A BIBLE CONCORDANCE, and
A BIBLE TEXT-BOOK,	A BIBLICAL ATLAS,

all in one; saving the cost of these books, and the time in their use, it is an invaluable work to the teacher, preacher, Bible-class leader, and Bible student generally.

"A marvellous amount of information on every imaginable subject is given in these nicely bound and well got up volumes. At a glance you may get everything that is to be said upon the subject. It is not a book to save the trouble of thinking, but it is a great aid to thought. We know of no work of its kind more valuable."—*Bible Student.*

ELLIOT STOCK, 62, PATERNOSTER ROW, LONDON, E.C.

New Works Published by Elliot Stock.

Fcap. 8vo., bound in neat cloth, gilt lettered, price 2s. post free,

GREEN'S
Biblical & Theological Dictionary.

Consisting of 418 pages, nearly 100 Illustrations, Tables of Weights and Measures, and a beautiful full-page Engraving of the Tabernacle and Encampment in the Wilderness, &c. Twenty-ninth Thousand. A new edition, revised to the present time.

This Dictionary has occupied a leading position in the Sunday-schools of England for many years. Nearly Twenty-six Thousand copies have been sold at 3s. 6d. each. It is now supplied to teachers, clearly printed on good paper, neatly bound in cloth and gilt lettered on the following terms:—

  6 copies for £0 10 0
  12 ,, ... 0 19 0

A single copy sent post free for two shillings.

"A more useful, compact, and beautiful book of reference for our Sunday-school teachers cannot well be imagined. It is the very thing that has long been wanted for them."—*Bible Class Magazine.*

Fourth Thousand, fcap. 8vo., price 2s. 6d. post free,

Sure of Heaven.

A BOOK FOR THE DOUBTING AND ANXIOUS.

By THOMAS MILLS.

"Mr. Mills's book is, in our opinion, incomparably the best that has been published. An experienced Christian, who has to do with inquirers, could hardly do better than put this book into their hands."—*Literary World.*

ELLIOT STOCK, 62, PATERNOSTER ROW, LONDON, E.C.

www.ingramcontent.com/pod-product-compliance
Lightning Source LLC
Chambersburg PA
CBHW020406230426
43664CB00009B/1203